CAMPAIGN • 215

LENINGRAD 1941–44

The epic siege

ROBERT FORCZYK ILLUSTRATED BY PETER DENNIS

Series editors Marcus Cowper and Nikolai Bogdanovic

First published in Great Britain in 2009 by Osprey Publishing,
Midland House, West Way, Botley, Oxford OX2 0PH, UK
443 Park Avenue South, New York, NY 10016, USA
E-mail: info@ospreypublishing.com

A CIP catalogue record for this book is available from the British Library.

ISBN: 978 1 84603 441 1
E Book ISBN: 978 1 84908 107 8

Editorial by Ilios Publishing Ltd, Oxford, UK (www.iliospublishing.com)

Page layout by The Black Spot
Index by Fineline Editorial Services
Typeset in Myriad Pro and Sabon
Maps by the Bounford.com.
3D bird's-eye views by The Black Spot
Battlescene illustrations by Peter Dennis
Originated by PPS Grasmere Ltd
Printed in China through Worldprint

09 10 11 12 13   10 9 8 7 6 5 4 3 2 1

DEDICATION

This volume is dedicated to Major Douglas A. Zembiec, US Marines,
killed during combat operations near Baghdad, 10 May 2007.

ACKNOWLEDGEMENTS

I wish to thank Nik Cornish, Monika Geilen at the Bundesarchiv, Peter
Harrington (curator of the Anne S. K. Brown collection at Brown University),
Ted Nevill of TRH Pictures, HITM Photo Archives and the staff at the
National Archives and Research Administration (NARA) for their assistance
in assembling photographs for this volume.

ARTIST'S NOTE

Readers may care to note that the original paintings from which the
battlescene colour plate in this book was prepared is available for private
sale. All reproduction copyright whatsoever is retained by the Publishers.
All enquiries should be addressed to:

Peter Dennis, Fieldhead, The Park, Mansfield, Notts, NG18 2AT, UK

The Publishers regret that they can enter into no correspondence
upon this matter.

THE WOODLAND TRUST

Osprey Publishing are supporting the Woodland Trust, the UK's leading
woodland conservation charity, by funding the dedication of trees.

Key to military symbols

××××	××××	×××	××	×	III	II
Army Group	Army	Corps	Division	Brigade	Regiment	Battalion
I	●●●	●●	●	Infantry	Artillery	Cavalry
Company/Battery	Platoon	Section	Squad			
Airborne	Unit HQ	Air defence	Air Force	Air mobile	Air transportable	Amphibious
Anti-tank	Armour	Air aviation	Bridging	Engineer	Headquarters	Maintenance
Medical	Missile	Mountain	Navy	Nuclear, biological, chemical	Ordnance	Parachute
Reconnaissance	Signal	Supply	Transport movement	Rocket artillery	Air defence artillery	

Key to unit identification

Unit identifier · Parent unit · Commander
(+) with added elements
(−) less elements

FOR A CATALOGUE OF ALL BOOKS PUBLISHED BY OSPREY MILITARY
AND AVIATION PLEASE CONTACT:

Osprey Direct, c/o Random House Distribution Center,
400 Hahn Road, Westminster, MD 21157
Email: uscustomerservice@ospreypublishing.com

Osprey Direct, The Book Service Ltd, Distribution Centre,
Colchester Road, Frating Green, Colchester, Essex, CO7 7DW
E-mail: customerservice@ospreypublishing.com

www.ospreypublishing.com

CONTENTS

ORIGINS OF THE CAMPAIGN

City of Peter, stand in all your splendor, Stand invincible like Russia ...
Aleksandr Pushkin, The Bronze Horseman, 1833

OPPOSITE

Soldiers from the 115th Rifle Division hold a dugout in the Nevskaya Dubrovka bridgehead in November 1941. Holding this tiny bridgehead across the Neva cost the Leningrad Front an estimated 30,000 casualties over six months in 1941/42. (RIA Novosti)

The city of St Petersburg has loomed large in the Russian national consciousness since founded by Peter I in 1703. Under the tsars, St Petersburg became the capital of the Russian Empire for the next two centuries and it was expanded into a great cultural centre as well as a commercial hub for trade in the Baltic, which helped spur Russia's economy. Furthermore, the nearby naval base at Kronstadt was made the headquarters of the Russian Baltic Fleet. In March 1917, the Russian Revolution began in the capital and the city was considered the heart of the Bolshevik movement.

After the Russian Civil War was over, the city was renamed Leningrad in 1924 and it became a vital component of the new Soviet Union. By 1940, Leningrad had a population of 2.54 million, making it the fourth largest city in Europe and the second largest in the Soviet Union, after Moscow. Leningrad's factories produced about ten per cent of the Soviet Union's entire industrial output, including much of its high-quality steel and the new KV-1 heavy tank.

As war in Europe approached, Stalin resolved to safeguard Leningrad by pushing the Soviet Union's vulnerable border areas back as far as possible from the city. After Finland refused to sell part of the Karelian Isthmus adjoining the Leningrad Military District (LMD), Stalin ordered the Red

Leningrad civilians digging an anti-tank ditch in the autumn of 1941. The mass mobilization of civilian labour was vital to Leningrad's defence. (RIA Novosti)

Army to seize the land by force in November 1939. The Soviet invasion began disastrously for the poorly prepared Red Army units but by March 1940 the war-weary Finns conceded most of the Karelian Isthmus. Under the terms of the armistice, the Finnish border was pushed back over 100km from Leningrad. Next, Stalin moved against the pro-German Baltic republics. In June 1940, Soviet troops marched into Latvia, Lithuania and Estonia and all three republics were annexed into the Soviet Union as the Baltic Special Military District. After this, Stalin moved three armies with 440,000 troops into the former Baltic States, which seemed to secure Leningrad against any threats from the west.

Yet unknown to Stalin, Adolf Hitler had already decided that the time was ripe to begin the anti-communist war of extermination spelled out in *Mein Kampf*. While the early *Barbarossa* planning emphasized military objectives – Moscow and Kiev – Leningrad was not even identified as a major

target. However, Hitler was adamant that Leningrad should receive equal priority with Moscow and Kiev. In his view, Operation *Barbarossa* was an ideological crusade to smash a heathen religion – Bolshevism – not merely an operational advance to destroy the Red Army. In order for the long-term racial-political objectives of *Generalplan Ost* to succeed, the cradle of Bolshevism must be wiped from the face of the earth. Thus, Hitler revised *Barbarossa* to make Leningrad one of the three main axes of advance for the Wehrmacht and he mandated that the advance on Moscow would not occur until Leningrad and Kronstadt had been eliminated.

Soviet militiamen in hastily dug rifle pits along the Neva River on 10 September 1941. The militia played a critical – if self-sacrificing role – in slowing the German advance on Leningrad. (RIA Novosti)

In order to fulfil Hitler's goal of destroying Leningrad, the Oberkommando des Heeres (OKH) created Heeresgruppe Nord, under Generalfeldmarschall Ritter von Leeb. Heeresgruppe Nord consisted of Armeeoberkommandos (AOK) 16 and 18, and 4. Panzergruppe, a total of 475,000 troops in 28 divisions. Although Leeb's intermediate task was to destroy all Soviet forces in the Baltic region, his ultimate task was to eliminate Leningrad's industrial base and its population. The Germans expected to cover the 765km from the East Prussian border to the outskirts of Leningrad in about six to eight weeks and to capture the city by mid-August. Although Finnish cooperation was expected, it was not deemed critical to capture the city.

The opening moves by Heeresgruppe Nord in June–August 1941 are covered in Campaign 148: *Operation Barbarossa 1941 (2)* (Osprey Publishing Ltd: Oxford, 2005) and will not be repeated here. Suffice to say that pre-war Soviet assumptions were shattered in the opening days and seriously compromised Leningrad's ability to defend itself. The Soviet forces in the Baltic States were badly defeated in the first 18 days of *Barbarossa*, with most of their tanks and aircraft lost. Those few reserve units available in the LMD were committed piecemeal into the path of the onrushing German Panzers and were also decimated. On 9 July 1941, Pskov – only 252km from Leningrad – fell to the Germans. General-Lieutenant Markian M. Popov, commander of the LMD, hurredly tried to erect a new defensive line along the Luga River while Leningrad's Communist Party boss, Andrei Zhdanov, provided 30,000 civilian volunteers to help build the fieldworks. Zhdanov also made a mass appeal for civilian volunteers that provided 160,000 recruits to form eight people's militia divisions in July.

By using these hastily raised troops, Popov and his successor, Marshal Kliment E. Voroshilov, were able to fight a successful delay on the Luga River that stopped Heeresgruppe Nord's headlong advance towards Leningrad for nearly a month. By the time that the Germans finally overwhelmed the Luga Line on 16 August, Leningrad's defenders had built a series of dense fortified lines on the south-west approaches to the city. However, the German advance shifted eastwards, severing the Leningrad–Moscow rail line at Chudovo on 20 August. With Soviet forces in retreat, Leeb dispatched XXXIX AK (mot.) to encircle Leningrad from the south-east while massing the rest of Heeresgruppe Nord for a direct assault on the city.

CHRONOLOGY

1941

22 June	Operation *Barbarossa* begins.
29 June	The Leningrad Military Council (LMC) begins work on the Luga Line.
14 July	Reinhardt's XXXXI AK (mot.) seizes a bridgehead over the Luga River.
31 July	Finnish attacks force the Soviet 23rd Army to withdraw to a new line only 30km north of Leningrad.
8 August	Heeresgruppe Nord begins breakout from Luga River bridgeheads.
20 August	German forces sever the Moscow–Leningrad railway line at Chudovo.
24 August	Luga falls.
30 August	German XXXIX AK (mot.) captures Mga.
2 September	Finnish forces reach the 1939 borders.
4 September	German artillery begins shelling Leningrad.
8 September	Germans captures Shlissel'burg, completing encirclement of Leningrad.
8 September	First major Luftwaffe raids on Leningrad.
9 September	Zhukov arrives in Leningrad to replace Voroshilov as Leningrad Front commander. Reinhardt's XXXXI AK (mot.) begins attack on Leningrad's outer defences.
12 September	1. Panzer-Division captures Krasnoye Selo.
13 September	L AK captures Krasnogvardeisk.
16 September	German XXXVIII AK reaches the Gulf of Finland, cutting off Soviet 8th Army in Oranienbaum pocket.
17/18 September	Pushkin falls but 1. Panzer-Division stopped on Pulkovo Heights, only 12km from city.
10–26 September	Zhukov's First Siniavino Offensive with 54th Army fails.
8 November	Germans capture Tikhvin.
19 November	Meretskov counterattacks at Tikhvin.
22 November	First major truck convoy crosses Lake Ladoga on ice road to Leningrad.
8 December	Germans abandon Tikhvin under heavy pressure and retreat to Volkhov.
17 December	Meretskov takes command of the new Volkhov Front.

1942

6 January	The Volkhov Front begins the Lyuban winter counteroffensive to break the blockade.

15 March	German counterattacks isolate the Soviet 2nd Shock Army in the Volkhov swamps.
4–20 April	Major Luftwaffe attacks on the Red Banner Baltic Fleet.
25 June	Soviet resistance in the Volkhov pocket collapses.
23 July	Führer Directive 45 specifies capture of Leningrad by September.
27 August	Soviets begin Second Siniavino Offensive to break through to Leningrad.
21 September	Manstein launches pincer attack at Soviet penetration near Siniavino, which cuts off the bulk of 8th Army and 2nd Shock Army.

1943

12 January	Operation *Spark*, the Third Siniavino Offensive begins.
18 January	2nd Shock Army and 67th Army link up north of Siniavino, establishing a small land corridor to Leningrad.
10 February	Soviet 55th Army attacks the Spanish 250. Infanterie-Division at Krasny Bor and 54th Army attacks the German XXVIII AK intending to link up near Tosno, but neither attack achieves a breakthrough.
22 July	Soviet Fifth Siniavino Offensive fails to capture the Siniavino Heights.
15 September	Simoniak's 30th Guards Rifle Corps finally captures the Siniavino Heights.
1 October	The Germans abandon the Kirishi salient.
5 November	Soviets begin shifting 2nd Shock Army to the Oranienbaum bridgehead.

1944

14 January	2nd Shock Army begins breakout from Oranienbaum while 42nd attacks from Leningrad on 15 January.
19 January	Soviet spearheads link-up at Ropsha.
21 January	Mga is liberated.
26 January	Krasnogvardeisk is liberated.
27 January	German AOK 18 begins falling back without orders. This marks the end of the siege of Leningrad.
29 January	Hitler relieves Küchler and replaces him with Model.

OPPOSING PLANS

GERMAN

Leningrad was one of three priority objectives specified in the *Barbarossa* plan, but Hitler kept modifying how he wanted the Wehrmacht to deal with the city. Originally, Heeresgruppe Nord's mission was simply to capture the city by direct assault but when this developed more slowly than expected, Hitler began to change the plan. He issued Führer Directive 34 on 30 July 1941, which specified that Heeresgruppe Nord would encircle Leningrad and establish contact with the Finns. Growing more skittish as the prospect of a major city battle drew near, Hitler issued Führer Directive 35 on 6 September 1941, which enjoined Leeb to avoid a costly attack directly into the city but still envisioned the rapid fall of the city after it was encircled. At this point, the OKH informed Leeb that he would soon have to transfer 4. Panzergruppe and Fliegerkorps VIII to Heeresgruppe Mitte, which put a timetable on further German offensive action towards Leningrad. Without these formations, Leeb felt that his command was too weak to continue further offensive action and he settled into a siege.

Shortly thereafter, the OKH issued Directive No. 1a 1601/41 on 22 September 1941, entitled *Concerning the Future Existence of the city of Leningrad*, which stated that 'the Führer has decided to erase the city of Petersburg from the face of the earth. We have no interest in the preservation of even a part of the population of that city.' Leeb was ordered to 'raze' Leningrad with air and artillery bombardments, while the siege starved the population into submission. Both Hitler and the OKH expected Leningrad's defence to collapse before spring 1942.

Yet once it became clear that Leningrad was not going to collapse quickly, Heeresgruppe Nord became committed to a static defence of siege lines around the city as well as blocking positions on the Volkhov front to prevent a Soviet relief effort. In May 1942, the OKH resurrected offensive plans

German infantry on patrol on the Volkhov front. The swampy terrain around Leningrad was some of the worst on the Eastern Front and had a profound impact upon operations. (Nik Cornish at Stavka)

to speed up and increase the effects of the siege, but the preparations for *Nordlicht* were half-hearted and low priority. Indeed, Küchler preferred to conserve strength by remaining on the defence and defeat one Soviet relief effort after another, rather than risk a Pyrrhic victory fighting his way into a fortified city.

After September 1942, the siege continued mostly for symbolic reasons – so that Hitler could demonstrate that he still had the home of Bolshevism by the throat – but it no longer contributed to the Soviet Union's defeat or Germany's survival. Indeed, even the tangible aspects of the siege – deaths by starvation, bombing and shelling – dropped off dramatically after spring 1942, reducing the siege to a fig leaf for the lack of any real operational plan for Heeresgruppe Nord.

SOVIET

Before the war, the LMD was not responsible for defending the southern or western approaches to the city – that was the responsibility of the Baltic Special Military District. Instead, the LMD was focused on holding Karelia against Finnish attempts to regain their lost territories. In the event of a German attack, the Leningrad Military Council (LMC) – influenced by the London 'Blitz' – expected the main threat to be air raids. Nobody really expected German ground troops to reach Leningrad so, like Singapore, most of the city's defences were facing in the wrong direction.

Once Heeresgruppe Nord's rapid advance through the Baltic States invalidated pre-war planning, the LMC was forced to develop a new defence on the fly and they did it fairly well. The Luga River was quickly identified as an excellent place to stop the German advance and the local Communist Party leadership, the military leadership and the population responded with alacrity to the threat. Zhdanov's mobilization of the militia divisions and the civilian construction battalions was probably the crucial decision that saved Leningrad, since the reinforcements that Stavka sent were too little and too

Colonel Ivan F. Chernenko (left), commander of the Izhorsky militia battalion, in front of a BA-10 armoured car. The tenacity Leningrad's militia demonstrated in the autumn of 1941 made the Wehrmacht reluctant to engage in an urban battle to take the city. (Author's collection)

late to prevent the city's encirclement. After the siege began, the LMC – not Zhukov or the Stavka – made the crucial decisions that strengthened the defences of the city and laid the groundwork for the cross-lake logistics that just barely staved off the city's collapse.

From the beginning, the mission of the Volkhov Front was simply to break through the German front and lift the siege, but the execution proved beyond their means for 17 months. Coordinated joint offensives between the Leningrad and Volkhov fronts in order to prevent the Germans from shifting reserves in time proved to be far more difficult than expected and AOK 18 employed a classic use of interior lines. Although Meretskov and Govorov were capable of planning efficient set-piece offensives, their efforts were continually undermined by recurrent interference from Stalin as well as various Stavka and NKVD busybodies. Again and again, Meretskov was forced to conduct offensives without adequate logistic preparation, which resulted in costly failures. Yet when given adequate time to prepare, both fronts demonstrated that they were capable of penetrating German prepared defences and reaching operational objectives. Another underlying difficulty in planning the relief of Leningrad was that the Stavka kept trying to enlarge the goals of each offensive from merely achieving a link-up between the two fronts to the more grandiose task of encircling all or part of AOK 18. In trying to conduct deep envelopments, the Soviet relief armies inevitably found themselves at the end of long, narrow salients that the Germans could then snip off.

OPPOSING COMMANDERS

Generaloberst Georg Lindemann (1884–1963), commander of AOK 18 from 16 January 1942 to March 1944. Lindemann proved to be very adept at shifting his limited infantry resources from one threatened sector to the next, fighting a classic battle of interior lines. (Bundesarchiv, 183-L08017)

GERMAN

Generalfeldmarschall Wilhelm Ritter von Leeb (1876–1956), commander of Heeresgruppe Nord from the start of *Barbarossa* until 13 January 1942. Leeb joined the Bavarian Army as an artillery officer in 1895 and he served as a staff officer on both the Eastern and Western fronts in World War I. Retained in the post-war Reichsheer, Leeb was involved in suppressing Hitler's 1923 Beer Hall Putsch and in 1938, Hitler forced him into retirement as a result of the Blomberg–Fritsch affair. However, Leeb was reinstated eight months later as war approached. Leeb was a Catholic, old-school officer who was critical of the Nazi regime, though he willingly accepted a 250,000 RM gift from its leaders in September 1941. His overall battle command was professional but uninspired and he flinched when confronted with wave after wave of Soviet infantry attacks on the Volkhov front. When Leeb started discussing retreat, Hitler sacked him.

Generalfeldmarschall Georg Wilhelm von Küchler, commander of Heeresgruppe Nord from January 1942 to January 1944. Küchler was another artillery officer with over 40 years of service. At the start of the war he commanded AOK 3 in East Prussia, which attacked Danzig. He then took command of the newly formed AOK 18 and in May 1940 he led it into Holland and Belgium, culminating in the encirclement of the BEF at Dunkirk. Küchler was more politically acceptable to Hitler, since he had openly supported the Nazis since 1938. While not particularly imaginative, Küchler became an expert at using his interior lines of railways to shift battalions and regiments from one endangered sector to another. However, Küchler suffered the same fate as Leeb when he began to retreat without orders in the face of the Soviet breakout in January 1944. He was later convicted of war crimes at Nuremburg in 1948 and served three years in prison.

Generaloberst Georg Lindemann, commander of AOK 18 from 16 January 1942 to March 1944. Lindemann was a cavalry officer from Saxony and he served on both the Eastern and Western fronts in World War I, as well as in an anti-communist Freikorps after the war. Earlier in World War II, he commanded the 36. Infanterie-Division during the invasion of France in 1940 and then L AK during *Barbarossa* in 1941. Lindemann ended the war as commander of German forces in Denmark.

Oberst Maximilian Wengler fought as a junior infantry officer on the Western Front in World War I. He left the army after the war and became an

insurance salesman but returned as a reserve officer at the start of World War II. Wengler fought as a battalion commander in Infanterie-Regiment 40 of the 227. Infanterie-Division in Holland in May 1940. Sent to the Leningrad front in December 1941, Wengler took command of Grenadier-Regiment 366 in late 1942 and successfully defended the approaches to the Siniavino Heights against massive Soviet attacks for the next year. After the retreat from Leningrad, Wengler conducted a skilful defence at Narva that stopped the Soviet advance with heavy losses and he was given command of the 227. Infanterie-Division. Wengler was one of only 159 members of the Wehrmacht to receive the Knight's Cross with Oak Leaves and Swords, owing to his repeated dogged defences against long odds. He was killed in action at Pillau on 25 April 1945. If Simoniak was the Red Army's unstoppable force, Wengler was the Wehrmacht's immovable object.

SOVIET

All decisions affecting the defence of Leningrad were in the hands of the LMC, which consisted of local Communist Party chief Andrei Zhdanov, the military commander of the LMD or front and several lesser figures. The LMC exercised command from an underground facility at the Smolny Institute – Lenin's old headquarters – on the east side of the city.

General-Lieutenant Markian M. Popov (1902–69) commanded the Leningrad Front at the start of the war, but was reduced to chief of staff when **Marshal Kliment Voroshilov** (1881–1969) arrived. Voroshilov has been dubbed as 'incompetent' but he displayed a rock-solid determination that helped the defence to solidify during the critical days leading up to the siege. Leningrad Communist Party chief **Andrei Zhdanov** (1896–1948) also played a critical role in organizing the defence of Leningrad, including mobilizing the population to help construct fieldworks, establishing the militia divisions and setting up the logistic lines across Lake Ladoga that kept the city alive. Zhdanov became a victim of Kremlin in-fighting after the war and his contribution to Leningrad's defence was minimized by Soviet sources.

General-Lieutenant Mikhail S. Khozin commanded the Leningrad Front from 23 October 1941 to June 1942. Khozin previously commanded the Leningrad Front in 1938, so he was familiar with the area. At the start of the war he was commandant of the Frunze Military Academy but was recalled

General Kirill A. Meretskov (1897–1968), commander of the Volhkov Front in 1941–44 and the man ultimately held responsible by Stalin for the relief of Leningrad. Meretskov was a gifted staff officer but his performance was undermined by his rival Zhukov and political interference from Stalin. (Author's collection)

to be Popov's chief of staff. When Zhukov arrived in Leningrad, he sent Khozin to organize the 54th Army on the Volkhov, but after Zhukov left, the Stavka recalled Khozin to take command in Leningrad. Khozin commanded the Leningrad garrison during the worst phase of the siege and should be credited not only with improving the city's defences, but conducting as many aggressive local counterattacks as his meagre resources allowed. Khozin was unable to coordinate properly the Leningrad and Volkhov fronts when his authority was expanded and he was relieved of command by Stalin after Vlasov's surrender in June 1942.

General Kirill Afanasievich Meretskov served as commander of the Volkhov Front from December 1941 to February 1944 and was the officer principally responsible for planning and conducting the relief of Leningrad. Meretskov was a draft-dodger during World War I and joined the Communist Party and Red Guards in 1917. Even though he had no formal military training, he served successfully as a staff officer during the Russian Civil War and the Russo-Polish War. Rising rapidly, Meretskov was made a brigade commander in 1922, sent to train in Germany in 1931 and in 1936 he went to Spain as an adviser. He helped to plan the Republican counteroffensive at the battle of Guadalajara in March 1937, which inflicted 6,000 casualties on the Italians and prevented the encirclement of Madrid. After his successful performance in Spain, Meretskov returned to the USSR and was commanding the LMD at the beginning of the disastrous Soviet invasion of Finland in November 1939. After his victory on the Mannerheim Line, General Meretskov was made a Hero of the Soviet Union and Chief of the General Staff, but was replaced by Zhukov in January 1941. In June 1941, Meretskov was running the training section in the Stavka and two days after the German invasion began, he was arrested by the NKVD because of his personal friendship with General Dmitri Pavlov, commander of the Western Front, who had been recalled to Moscow and executed. Meretskov was accused of being a traitor and tortured for two months in the Lubyanka Prison; he was repeatedly beaten about the head with rubber truncheons and eventually signed a written confession.

However, once Leningrad was encircled Stalin recognized that he needed Meretskov's battlefield skill and he was released on 8 September and sent to take charge of the 7th Army on the Svir River front and then the 4th Army near Tikhvin in November. Given command of the Volkhov Front, Meretskov spent the next 17 months trying to batter his way through to relieve Leningrad. Later, he commanded the Karelian Front during the Soviet offensive against the Finns in June 1944, was promoted to marshal in October 1944 and then led the 1st Far Eastern Front into Manchuria in August 1945. Meretskov was an excellent set-piece battlefield commander – one of the best the Soviets had – but he was constantly forced to act prematurely owing to fear that any hesitation to act would result in being sent back to the Lubyanka Prison.

General-Lieutenant Leonid Aleksandrovich Govorov, commander of Leningrad Front from April 1942 to July 1945. Govorov was commissioned an artillery officer in the Russian Imperial Army in early 1917 and initially joined the Whites in the Civil War before switching to the Red Army. Owing to this connection with the Whites, Govorov narrowly avoided the purges. During the Russo-Finnish War, he served as Meretskov's chief of staff in 7th Army and coordinated the massive artillery bombardment that enabled the breakthrough of the Mannerheim Line. During the 1941 campaign, he served

as a senior artillery adviser to Zhukov during the defence of Moscow and commanded the 5th Army during the Soviet Winter Counteroffensive that liberated Mozhaisk. In Leningrad, Govorov was mainly responsible for strengthening the counterbattery effort that helped to reduce the German bombardment of the city, and his close cooperation with Meretskov resulted in the successful relief of the city. Govorov and Meretskov usually worked well together, which vastly improved coordination between the two fronts.

General-Lieutenant Ivan F. Fediuninskiy served in a number of key command roles on the Leningrad and Volkhov fronts in 1941–44. Fediuninskiy joined the Red Army in 1919 and he served mostly in the Far East in the inter-war years. He got his big break in August 1939, commanding a motorized regiment as part of Zhukov's counterattack that encircled the Japanese 23rd Infantry Division at the battle of Khalkin-Gol. This coup brought Fediuninskiy to Zhukov's attention and he was awarded the Hero of the Soviet Union. In June 1941, Fediuninskiy was commanding the 15th Rifle Corps in the Ukraine but was brought back to Moscow to organize one of the reserve armies. Instead, Zhukov grabbed him and took him to Leningrad as

his deputy, then put him in charge of the 42nd Army when it appeared that 4. Panzergruppe might break through at Pulkovo. Shortly thereafter, Fediuninskiy took over the 54th Army on the Volkhov Front and his offensive in March 1942 succeeded in creating the Pogost'e salient. He also played a key role during Operation *Star*, but was badly wounded by enemy mortar fire on 20 January 1943. Returning to duty later in 1943, he took command of the 2nd Shock Army and led it successfully in the breakout from Oranienbaum in January 1944. Fediuninskiy was something of a pinch-hitter for the Red Army, commanding no less than six armies in four years and being a protégé of Zhukov made him less vulnerable than Meretskov or Govorov to pressure from the Stavka or NKVD.

General-Major Nikolai P. Simoniak, commander of the elite 30th Guards Rifle Corps in 1943/44, which spearheaded the breakthrough in Operation *Spark*, fought the Spaniards at Krasny Bor, captured the Siniavino Heights and led the breakout from Leningrad. Earlier, Simoniak commanded the 8th Rifle Brigade in the Hango Peninsula against the Finns in June–November 1941. After his brigade was evacuated to Kronstadt, it was transformed into the 136th Rifle Division in 1942, and then redesignated the 63rd Guards Rifle Division in 1943. Simoniak's unit saw more action than any other Soviet unit in the siege of Leningrad and he was regarded as a tough, aggressive commander who was regularly given the hardest assignments and succeeded. Nor was Simoniak willing to be bullied by Zhukov into wasting his men's lives; when Zhukov accused him of cowardice and tried to push him into a premature attack on the Siniavino Heights, Simoniak deliberately rebuffed him. Simoniak later commanded the 3rd Shock Army in 1944/45 but was prematurely retired in 1948.

OPPOSING FORCES

GERMAN

Once Hitler decided to besiege Leningrad and transferred 4. Panzergruppe to Heeresgruppe Mitte, Heeresgruppe Nord became a resource-poor force that relied heavily upon a few elite formations and superior defensive tactics to hold off Soviet relief efforts for the next three years. The primary German formations involved in the siege were AOK 18 and Luftflotte I.

Tanks and assault guns

The only armour available in the Leningrad area for most of 1942 was the relatively weak 12. Panzer-Division and a mixed *Kampfgruppe* of 8. Panzer-Division. The 12. Panzer-Division was so ruined by the losses suffered in the battle of Tikhvin that, even by June 1942, it could field only a single Panzer battalion of 41 tanks. Throughout most of the early battles of 1942, AOK 18 relied for anti-tank defence on a small number of StuG III assault guns from StuG-Batterie 667 and StuG-Abteilung 185, as well as the corps-level Panzerjäger-Abteilung 563, which received Marders in 1943. In late August 1942, AOK 18 was reinforced with 1./schwere Panzer-Abteilung 502 – the first Tiger tank unit operationally deployed in the Wehrmacht. Although the unit remained at company strength until July 1943, with only one to nine

A Tiger tank from schwere Panzer-Abteilung 502. Although few in number, the Tigers played a major role in stopping the Soviet offensives around Leningrad in 1943. (Nik Cornish at Stavka)

Tigers operational at one time, it played a major role in stiffening the German defence around Siniavino. During January–February 1943, this one company was credited with accounting for 25 per cent of all Soviet tanks knocked out by AOK 18. In July 1943, the rest of the battalion arrived at Leningrad and the number of operational Tigers jumped up to 30. Constantly in action, the unit gradually built up a cadre of very skilled and experienced crews, such as Otto Carius who had over 50 'kills'. Until late 1943, s.Pz.Abt. 502 was the bane of Soviet tankers on the Leningrad front.

SS volunteer units

Even before *Barbarossa*, the Waffen-SS had begun forming several legions of non-German volunteers to participate in the 'crusade against Bolshevism', although their primary contribution was expected to be as props in German propaganda efforts. However, the urgent need for infantry replacements resulted in these volunteer units being thrown into fierce action on the Volkhov in early 1942. The first to arrive was the SS-Freiwilligen Legion 'Flandern', followed by the SS-Freiwilligen Legion 'Niederlande', the SS-Freiwilligen Legion 'Norwegen' and 2. SS-Infanterie-Brigade (mot.), which was formed from Dutch and Norwegian volunteers. Altogether, these formations contributed seven infantry battalions to German operations around Leningrad in 1942/43 and their combat performance on the Volkhov was quite good. However, these units were also very fragile since they could not replace heavy losses and were quickly burnt out in attritional battles. For example, the Legion 'Flandern' was reduced from 1,100 men to less than 400 in just three months of combat and even after slowly rebuilding throughout 1942, it was virtually destroyed at Krasny Bor in March 1943. Furthermore, the initial enthusiasm of the volunteers began to wane after Stalingrad and it became clear that Germany was losing the war, which greatly reduced the flow of replacements. All of the original legions were withdrawn in the spring of 1943, but their cadres were joined with *Volksdeutsche* recruits to form the 11. SS-Freiwilligen-Panzergrenadier-Division 'Nordland' (composed of 33 per cent Germans, 46 per cent *Volksdeutsche* from Romania, ten per cent Danes, five per cent Norwegians and six per cent others). In addition, the SS had gathered so many Latvian volunteers that they formed them into 2.

SS-Standartenführer Otto Gieseke (1891–1958), commander of SS-Polizei-Schützen-Regiment 1, in the forward trenches near Kolpino in October 1941. The SS-Polizei-Division proved to be a very formidable opponent and it fought on the Leningrad front for almost the entire duration of the siege. (HITM Archives)

Lettische SS-Freiwilligen-Brigade. Both units were sent to join III SS-Panzerkorps at Leningrad in December 1943. Overall, the SS volunteer units played a much greater role in the desperate battles fought around Leningrad than their small size would suggest.

However, not all the SS units around Leningrad were composed of high-quality volunteers. In late October 1941, Obergruppenführer Friedrich Jeckeln arrived in Riga with a battalion of SS police and on 30 November his unit conducted the infamous 'Rumbula massacre' outside Riga, murdering over 27,000 civilians. As Higher SS and Police Leader for North Russia, Jeckeln also was in charge of Einsatzgruppe A operations around Leningrad. However, in order to detach regular units from the siege lines around Leningrad to deal with the Lyuban Offensive, AOK 18 ordered Jeckeln to form a Kampfgruppe from his SS police and Latvian Schuma (security) auxiliaries and to join L AK from May–November 1942. This was probably the only time on the Eastern Front where SS 'special action' troops were used in the front line for any length of time.

Defensive tactics

Prior to *Barbarossa*, German defensive doctrine stressed the concept of 'elastic defence' conducted in depth, but none of this was applicable on the Leningrad front. Since Hitler forbade all but minor tactical withdrawals, there could be no trading space and there were too few infantry left to establish a continuous defence, never mind a defence in depth. Nor were there sufficient reserves to support a mobile defence. Thus, Lindemann was forced to rely on strongpoint defences that were tied to holding key terrain, backed up by powerful artillery. As a buffer, German divisions built a security zone that extended two to four kilometres back from the forward line of contact; this zone had platoon- or company-sized strongpoints equipped with heavy machine guns and mortars. The security zone was not strong enough to stop a major Soviet attack and, since it didn't even hold a continuous front, it was quite possible for the Soviets to advance through this zone. The real German defences, battalion-sized strongpoints with some artillery and anti-tank guns, were located three to five kilometres further back and usually could not be seen by Soviet artillery forward observers. These strongpoints controlled the handful of available mobility corridors and were strong enough to resist division-sized attacks. A key strongpoint, like Spasskaya Polist held by Kampfbataillon Ehrenpfordt in February 1942, had 789 troops, 68 machine guns, four 81mm mortars, five 37mm anti-tank guns, two 20mm flak guns, two 75mm infantry guns and a single PzKpfw III tank. A barrier of Teller mines and barbed wire further protected this strongpoint.

When Soviet rifle units conducted an attack, the security zone provided early warning and helped to disrupt their momentum, although most German troops in these positions were eventually overwhelmed. By the time that Soviet rifle units reached the main strongpoints, they usually got stuck in the obstacle belt and were then pounded to pieces by German mortars and MG42 fire. As time went on, the Germans continued to harden these forward strongpoints with bunkers and trenches, making them more and more resistant to Soviet artillery and air attacks. Even when surrounded, German strongpoints around Siniavino proved that they could hold out for days. Once Soviet offensives ran out of steam, German corps commanders then used the surviving strongpoints as jumping-off positions for pincer counterattacks that often ended up encircling the exhausted Soviet spearhead units.

Artillery bombardment capabilities

Armeeoberkommando 18's higher artillery command, Harko 303 led by Generalleutnant Hans Kratzert, was responsible for directing the bombardment of Leningrad, but initially its capabilities were very limited since the *Barbarossa* plan had envisioned taking the city with a rapid *coup de main*, rather than as part of a siege. Owing to the distance from German lines to the city, only heavy artillery possessed the range to bombard targets inside Leningrad effectively, although medium artillery could strike targets in the southern suburbs. Kratzert's best weapons were the six 21cm mortars of schwere Artillerie-Abteilung 768 and the eight 24cm cannons of I and II/Artillerie-Regiment 84, which were located in the woods near the Peterhof. During the period September–December 1941, German artillery fired 40,154 rounds into the city, inflicting several thousand civilian casualties. German artillery fire against the city was persistent – often lasting for hours – but it failed to destroy any key targets. For example, the Hermitage Museum was hit repeatedly, but the damage was superficial. Targets such as the Kirov and Bolshevik tank plants were hit repeatedly but still continued to repair damaged tanks. Most of the guns bombarding the city centre were in fact, captured French 155mm guns, which hurled a 43kg high-explosive shell with only a seven kilogram bursting charge. Kratzert also formed a schwere Flachfeuer Gruppe (heavy flat-trajectory artillery group) to engage the Red Banner Baltic Fleet, which succeeded in damaging the cruiser *Petropavlovsk* and then sinking the training cruiser *Aurora* and three submarines. However, the German railway system in Russia was too overburdened in the winter of 1941/42 to send greater artillery resources to demolish Leningrad, so Kratzert was forced to make do with a relatively small artillery park and limited amounts of ammunition.

Gradually, the OKH sent more heavy artillery to reinforce AOK 18, but even in January 1942 Harko 303 had fewer than 40 heavy guns. The main reinforcements consisted of two railway artillery batteries armed with two French-built 520mm guns and two 283mm 'Short Bruno' guns, although the 520mm guns were soon replaced with handier French-built 400mm rail guns. A battery of 17cm Kanone 18s, with a range out to 29.6km, was also sent to provide better counterbattery capabilities. Yet it was not until Operation *Nordlicht* became a serious possibility that the OKH began to provide Kratzert with the resources to inflict serious damage on Leningrad. A total of 12 super-heavy artillery batteries arrived in the Leningrad area in August, although most were kept in reserve to conserve their limited ammunition supply. Harko 303 gained three more French-built 40cm and 37cm railway guns, two 28cm K-5 railway guns, one 42cm Gamma mortar, one 355mm mortar, five Czech-built 305mm mortars and two French-built 24cm railway guns. In addition, the 80cm Dora gun and two 60cm Karl mortars were scheduled to join Harko 303 as soon as possible. Küchler was unsure how best to use this super-heavy artillery, since they had enough ammunition for only one major attack. He seriously considered concentrating most of the guns against Kronstadt, including 'Dora' which was specifically designed for cracking fortresses. If Kronstadt's coastal guns and flak could be neutralized, a direct assault to eliminate the Oranienbaum bridgehead would become practical.

However, the Soviet offensive in August 1942 pre-empted *Nordlicht* and Küchler decided to keep most of his heavy guns in reserve. Both 'Dora' and the two Karl mortars arrived south of Leningrad but were not used and sent back to Germany in late 1942. Indeed, the bombardment of Leningrad slacked off in the last half of 1942 as Kratzert conserved ammunition for an offensive that never happened. By spring 1943, Kratzert resumed a more intensive bombardment of Leningrad, firing an average of 85 rounds per day, but this dropped off to 30 rounds per day after the summer of 1943. During the period 10–30 April 1943, Kratzert's guns fired 2,912 rounds into Leningrad, of which less than five per cent were 28cm, six per cent were 21cm, 41 per cent were 17cm and 48 per cent were 15 to 12cm. Soviet counterbattery fire sent back over 4,000 rounds at the German artillery, but succeeded in destroying only one French 155mm howitzer and damaging two other guns, as well as inflicting 12 casualties. The best German weapons for bombarding Leningrad were the handful of 28cm K-5 guns, which could fire a 255kg shell into the city from well beyond the range of Soviet counterbattery fire, but these weapons had only enough ammunition to fire occasionally.

Luftwaffe ground units

Beginning in the winter of 1941/42, the OKH decided to use Luftwaffe ground troops to reinforce Heeresgruppe Nord, since most army replacements were going to Heeresgruppe Mitte and Heeresgruppe Süd. The first Luftwaffe units to arrive at Leningrad were five battalions of 7. Flieger-Division, which were put into the line near Shlissel'burg on 30 September 1941. The *Fallschirmjäger* helped to repel repeated Soviet counterattacks across the Neva but in the course of six weeks they suffered a crippling 2,782 casualties and they were withdrawn in mid-December 1941. In November 1942, the first of six Luftwaffe field divisions arrived in Heeresgruppe Nord, followed by III Luftwaffe-Feld-Korps, which took over the quiet Oranienbaum sector. Leadership was weak in many of the Luftwaffe divisions, although the army transferred a few seasoned officers such as Generalleutnant Hellmuth Reymann from 212. Infanterie-Division to take over 13. Luftwaffe-Feld-Division. Ultimately, the Luftwaffe field divisions proved to be an expensive gap-filler that were adequate to hold quiet sectors but which could not conduct effective defences against the kind of firepower that the Red Army wielded by 1944.

SOVIET

The main Soviet formations involved in the siege of Leningrad were the 42nd and 55th armies, and the Neva Operational Group (NOG) – which later became the 67th Army. The 23rd Army held the Karelian Front in 1941–44, but this formation saw little action during the siege owing to Finnish inactivity. Of the four armies in Leningrad, the 55th was the largest and had up to half the active units. Although these formations had the equivalent of about 20 rifle divisions in early 1942, the actual number of troops was probably only about 95,000, not including naval infantry or VVS/PVO personnel.

Shock groups

In January 1942, Zhukov directed Soviet commanders to employ 'shock groups' – concentrating all combat resources on narrow fronts – to blast through German fortified lines. Unfortunately for Leningrad, the Red Army often interpreted this directive as crowding large masses of infantry into penetration corridors that were only one to two kilometres wide, which made great targets for German artillery. At first, Meretskov's shock groups were

A militia unit formed from Kirov Factory workers heads to the front on 6 July 1941. These troops were formed into the 2nd Leningrad Militia Division (DNO), which suffered heavy losses in a vain effort to hold the Luga Line. The survivors were redesignated the 85th Rifle Division and spent most of the siege in the 55th Army. (Author's collection)

regimental-sized and consisted mostly of riflemen, who were expected to tackle MG42 bunkers, surrounded with wire and mines, with only their bolt-action Mosin-Nagant rifles and a few grenades. The result was one rifle company after another mown down for negligible gains. Although Soviet shock groups were strong enough to push through the outer German security zone, their inability to overcome fortified strongpoints severely limited Soviet offensive capabilities in 1942. However, by 1943 Meretskov had learned from his mistakes and began to organize smaller, better armed assault detachments. For Operation *Spark* in January 1943, a typical Soviet assault detachment had 127 soldiers, including a scout squad, a sapper platoon for obstacle clearance, a section of 45mm anti-tank guns to reduce bunkers, a rifle platoon reinforced with a section of automatic riflemen and a team of artillery forward observers. Once the Red Army shock groups could reliably demolish a German company-sized strongpoint, Soviet offensives gained the ability to affect real penetrations.

Armour

The large number of KV-1 and KV-2 heavy tanks available on the Leningrad Front played a major role in saving the city in September 1941. Although Heeresgruppe Nord had already encountered Soviet heavy tanks in Lithuania, they had been employed individually and without infantry support, enabling the Germans to overcome them eventually, albeit with difficulty. However, near Pulkovo, for the first time 4. Panzergruppe encountered a battalion-sized unit of KV-1 and KV-2 tanks, supported by infantry, and were shocked. German Panzerjäger troops, armed with 37mm Pak 36 guns, could not stop these behemoths, nor could German PzKpfw III tanks effectively engage large numbers of them. In short, the Wehrmacht in September 1941 had no easy answer on how to dislodge that type of opponent. Eventually, the Germans found an answer to the KV tank with the arrival of hollow charges, Teller mines and the 75mm Pak 40 anti-tank gun in late 1941. By 1942, neither KV or T-34 tanks could operate with impunity against German *Panzerjäger* and Soviet armour played a relatively minor role in most of the subsequent efforts

to relieve the city. Unlike other Soviet offensives, the swampy terrain and narrow mobility corridors around Leningrad prevented the Red Army from using armour in mass formations. Instead, tanks often had to advance in column along wooded trails, which made them vulnerable to mines and well-sited German anti-tank guns.

Coastal artillery and the counterbattery corps

Leningrad and Kronstadt were protected by an impressive array of coastal batteries and forts, some of which were also capable of supporting the ground defence. Kronstadt itself had a large number of batteries, ranging from 6in. up to 12in. guns, but the most dangerous positions to the Germans were located on the northern shores of the Oranienbaum bridgehead. A coastal fort known as Krasnaya Gorka (Red Hill) had eight 12in. and three 6in. guns surrounded by two lines of land defences with concrete bunkers. There were also two railway guns operating near Krasnaya Gorka, the 356mm TM-3-12 gun and the 180mm TM-1-180 gun, as well as the armoured trains *Baltietz* and *Za Rodinu*. Further west, Battery Shepelov had two twin 14in. guns and Fort Pulkova had two twin 8in. guns. In September 1941, the 356mm railway gun fired 568 rounds at German forces attacking Leningrad and the Kronstadt coastal guns added another 9,000 rounds in the same period. Soviet coastal batteries could strike targets as distant as Krasnoye Selo and the strength of their defences explains in part why the Oranienbaum bridgehead survived. The Luftwaffe was never able to silence these batteries since anti-aircraft guns ringed them and they were a constant nuisance to AOK 18's left flank.

Early in the siege, the Soviets realized that they needed a counterbattery artillery group to respond to German bombardments or the city would be gradually reduced to ruins. The Leningrad Counterbattery Artillery Corps was established under the command of General-Major Georgii F. Odintsov, but the limited amount of artillery ammunition prevented this group from having much effect on the German guns in 1942. By 1943, Odintsov had a total of 90 152mm ML-20 howitzers and 32 122mm M1931/37 guns under his command, and enough ammunition to respond in kind to German

A battery of Soviet 152mm M1909/30 howitzers deployed in reverse slope firing positions. These elderly weapons were modernized in the 1930s but their limited range of only 8.8km was severely outclassed by the German 15cm s.FH18 howitzer, which had a range of 13.3km. (Fonds of the RGKFD, Krasnogorsk)

bombardments. Soviet artillery had better range and fired heavier shells than the bulk of the German corps-level artillery that opposed them, but Odintsov was unable to neutralize the longer-range German railway artillery units. Nevertheless, the creation of the Counterbattery Artillery Corps helped to limit the bombardment damage inflicted on Leningrad by causing German gunners to concentrate more on camouflage and survivability moves, rather than pounding away uninterrupted at the city.

The Red Banner Baltic Fleet and naval infantry

The Red Banner Baltic Fleet (Krasnoznamyonnyy Baltiyskiy Flot, KBF) suffered heavy losses during the evacuation of Tallinn on 28/29 August, but by the beginning of the siege of Leningrad it still had enough warships left to provide considerable naval gunfire support to Soviet ground troops. The heavyweights were the battleships *Marat* and *October Revolution*, each with 12 305mm guns that could hurl 470kg high-explosive shells out to 24km, and the heavy cruisers *Kirov* and *Maxim Gorky*, each with nine 180mm guns that could fire 97kg shells out to 33km. Additionally, the incomplete heavy cruiser *Petropavlovsk* (ex-*Lutzow*), purchased from Germany in 1940, had two operational 8in. gun turrets. The KBF also had seven operational *Gnevny*-class destroyers, as well as a number of smaller warships. In addition, the KBF operated a railway battery with four 180mm guns, as well as a naval test range near Toksovo that had a single 406mm gun, a 356mm gun and two 305mm guns. Once the Germans mined the Gulf of Finland, the KBF could not risk moving around much and the fuel-oil shortage virtually immobilized the largest warships. Nevertheless, even from their anchorages the Soviet warships could bombard targets around Pushkin and Krasnoye Selo. On the receiving end, the Germans found the Soviet heavy naval gunfire discouraging but not very accurate. Amazingly, less than 30 per cent of Soviet naval gunfire used an observer – often it was just fired at area targets – which greatly diminished its effectiveness. Yet the KBF fired over 25,000 rounds against German ground troops during September 1941, which played a major role in stopping the enemy's final lunge toward the city.

During the course of the siege of Leningrad, the KBF provided over 125,000 sailors to fight in ground units, comprising nine rifle brigades, one ski regiment, 38 separate battalions and 32 artillery batteries. The 1st Naval Rifle Brigade played a crucial role in holding Leningrad in 1941 but was virtually destroyed, while the 2nd, 5th and 6th naval rifle brigades helped to hold the Oranienbaum bridgehead. The 4th Naval Rifle Brigade was tasked with defending the ice road over Lake Ladoga in the winter of 1941/42 and spent virtually the entire winter on the ice.

Ladoga Flotilla

The Ladoga Flotilla was formed in October 1939 to assist in the Russo-Finnish War and it proved to be a critical logistical asset that kept Leningrad alive in the autumn of 1941 and summer of 1942. The flotilla also helped to save elements of the 23rd Army in Karelia that would otherwise have surrendered to the Finns. Once the city was encircled, the commander of the flotilla, Captain Vladimir S. Cherokov, set up his headquarters in Novaya Ladoga and began to organize supply convoys across the lake in September–November 1941. Once the winter ice shut down naval traffic on the lake, Zhdanov ordered Leningrad's extensive shipbuilding facilities to construct a large number of vessels to augment the flotilla in the following year's efforts. By the summer of

1942, the Ladoga Flotilla had a dozen small warships, nine freighters and over 80 barges, which enabled it to transport over 5,000 tons of cargo per day across the lake. Although the Luftwaffe was able to sink a number of vessels in the flotilla, they never came close to shutting down its operations.

ORDERS OF BATTLE

2 JANUARY 1942

GERMAN

AOK 18 (Generaloberst Georg Wilhelm von Küchler)

I AK (General der Infanterie Kuno von Both)

    11. Infanterie-Division

    21. Infanterie-Division

    254. Infanterie-Division

    291. Infanterie-Division (-)

    SS-Infanterie-Regiment 9

    I/Panzer-Regiment 203

    One mixed battalion each from 8. Panzer-Division and 12. Panzer-Division

XXVI AK (General der Artillerie Albert Wodrig)

    93. Infanterie-Division

    212. Infanterie-Division

    217. Infanterie-Division

XXVIII AK (General der Artillerie Herbert Loch)

    1. Infanterie-Division

    96. Infanterie-Division

    223. Infanterie-Division

    227. Infanterie-Division

    269. Infanterie-Division

    Sicherungs-Regiment 374

    Panzer-Bataillon 'Wuchenauer' (8. Panzer-Division)

    Bataillon von Muller (12. Panzer-Division)

    Panzerjäger-Bataillon 563

L AK (General der Kavallerie Georg Lindemann)

    58. Infanterie-Division

    121. Infanterie-Division

    122. Infanterie-Division

    SS-Polizei-Division

SOVIET

Leningrad Front (Gen.Lt. Mikhail Khozin)

23rd Army (Gen.Lt. Aleksandr Cherepanov)

    123rd Rifle Division

    142nd Rifle Division

    291st Rifle Division

42nd Army (Gen.Lt. Ivan Nikolaev)

    13th Rifle Division

    189th Rifle Division

    21st NKVD Rifle Division

55th Army (Gen.Lt. Vladimir Sviridov)

    11th Rifle Division

    43rd Rifle Division

    56th Rifle Division

    70th Rifle Division

    72nd Rifle Division

    85th Rifle Division

    86th Rifle Division

    90th Rifle Division

    125th Rifle Division

    177th Rifle Division

    268th Rifle Division

Neva Operational Group (NOG)

    1st NKVD Rifle Division

    11th Rifle Brigade

    4th Naval Infantry Brigade

Coastal Operational Group in Oranienbaum

    48th Rifle Division

    168th Rifle Division

    2nd Naval Infantry Brigade

    5th Naval Infantry Brigade

54th Army (Gen.Maj. Ivan Fediuninskiy)

    3rd Guards Rifle Division

    80th Rifle Division

    115th Rifle Division

    128th Rifle Division

    198th Rifle Division

    281st Rifle Division

    285th Rifle Division

    286th Rifle Division

    294th Rifle Division

    311th Rifle Division

    1st Mountain Rifle Brigade

    6th Naval Infantry Brigade

    16th Tank Brigade

    122nd Tank Brigade

Front reserves
- 10th Rifle Division
- 20th NKVD Rifle Division
- 123rd Tank Brigade
- 124th Tank Brigade

1 JANUARY 1944

GERMAN

AOK 18 (Generaloberst Georg Lindemann)
III SS-Panzer-Korps (SS-Obergruppenführer Felix Steiner)
- 11. SS-Panzergrenadier-Division 'Nordland'
- 4. SS-Brigade (mot.) 'Nederland'
- 9. Luftwaffe-Feld-Division
- 10. Luftwaffe-Feld-Division
- Kampfgruppe SS-Polizei

XXVI AK (General der Infanterie Martin Grase)
- 61. Infanterie-Division
- 212. Infanterie-Division
- 227. Infanterie-Division
- 254. Infanterie-Division

L AK (General der Infanterie Wilhelm Wegener)
- 126. Infanterie-Division
- 170. Infanterie-Division
- 215. Infanterie-Division

LIV AK (General der Infanterie Otto Sponheimer)
- 11. Infanterie-Division
- 24. Infanterie-Division
- 225. Infanterie-Division

SOVIET

Leningrad Front (Gen.Lt. Leonid Govorov)
23rd Army (Gen.Lt. Aleksandr Cherepanov)
- 10th Rifle Division
- 92nd Rifle Division
- 142nd Rifle Division

42nd Army (Colonel-General Ivan Maslennikov)
- 30th Guards Rifle Corps (Gen.Maj. Nikolai Simoniak)
  - 45th Guards Rifle Division
  - 63rd Guards Rifle Division
  - 64th Guards Rifle Division
- 108th Rifle Corps
  - 196th Rifle Division
  - 224th Rifle Division
  - 314th Rifle Division
- 109th Rifle Corps
  - 72nd Rifle Division
  - 109th Rifle Division
  - 125th Rifle Division
- 110th Rifle Corps
  - 56th Rifle Division
  - 85th Rifle Division
  - 86th Rifle Division
- 189th Rifle Division
- 18th Breakthrough Artillery Division
- 23rd Breakthrough Artillery Division
- 1st Tank Brigade
- 220th Tank Brigade
- 31st Guards Tank Regiment
- 46th Guards Tank Regiment
- 49th Guards Tank Regiment

67th Army (Gen.Lt. Vladimir Sviridov)
- 116th Rifle Corps
  - 13th Rifle Division
  - 46th Rifle Division
  - 376th Rifle Division
- 117th Rifle Corps
  - 120th Rifle Division
  - 123rd Rifle Division
  - 201st Rifle Division
- 118th Rifle Corps
  - 124th Rifle Division
  - 128th Rifle Division
  - 268th Rifle Division
- 291st Rifle Division

2nd Shock Army (Gen.Lt. Ivan Fediuninskiy)
- 43rd Rifle Corps
  - 48th Rifle Division
  - 90th Rifle Division
  - 98th Rifle Division
- 122nd Rifle Corps
  - 11th Rifle Division
  - 131st Rifle Division
  - 168th Rifle Division
- 43rd Rifle Division
- 50th Rifle Brigade
- 48th Naval Rifle Brigade
- 71st Naval Rifle Brigade
- 152nd Tank Brigade

THE SIEGE OF LENINGRAD

The Iron ring around Leningrad has been closed.
OKH Communiqué, 7 September 1941

THE BLOCKADE BEGINS: SEPTEMBER–DECEMBER 1941

At the start of September 1941, Leeb hurled Hoepner's 4. Panzergruppe against the Soviet fortified town of Krasnogvardeisk, while Schmidt's XXXIX AK (mot.) continued its envelopment of Leningrad to the north-east. Soviet militia and Red Army units put up a valiant resistance at Krasnogvardeisk, which succeeded in buying more time for Leningrad's inner defences to harden. However, the Soviet situation deteriorated quickly when the Finns began their offensive into Karelia on 10 July and routed the Soviet 23rd Army, which fell back in disorder. Finnish forces pursued and by 2 September they reached the old 1939 border, but the Finnish Government had no desire to attack Leningrad and was satisfied that it had liberated its lost lands. Marshal Mannerheim ordered the six Finnish divisions in Karelia to shift to the defence, with some units within 32km of Leningrad. The battered 23rd Army had suffered over 40,000 casualties and the remaining divisions were reduced to about 30 per cent strength.

Although Hoepner was temporarily stymied by Krasnogvardeisk, Schmidt's motorized troops advanced into the vacuum south-east of Leningrad, capturing Lyuban and Tosno by 29 August and then Mga on 30

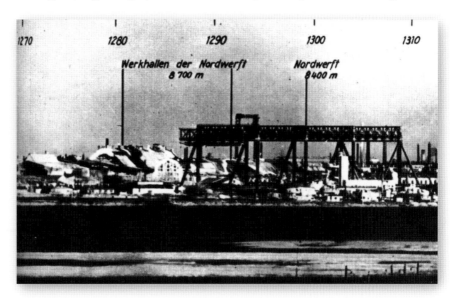

The Kirov Factory in Leningrad as seen from a German observation post, 8,400m away, on top of a rooftop in Uritsk. Although the plant was hit repeatedly, Soviet workers continued to operate in the plant throughout the siege. (Author's collection)

August. The loss of Mga was a disaster for the Soviets because it severed the last rail link between Leningrad and the outside world. Voroshilov committed his reserves and briefly recaptured the city, but German counterattacks routed them. On 31 August, the Stavka ordered the formation of two new armies to defend Leningrad: the 42nd Army (General-Lieutenant Fedor S. Ivanov) to defend the south-western approaches around Krasnoye Selo and Pushkin, and the 55th Army (General-Major Ivan G. Lazarev) to defend the eastern sector from Kolpino to Shlissel'burg. The 8th Army, gradually being pushed back towards Oranienbaum by AOK 18, would continue to hold the western approaches to the city. However, these armies consisted of only bits and pieces, not fully formed divisions.

Schmidt made the final push to Lake Ladoga with two *Kampfgruppen* from 126. Infanterie-Division, which captured the Siniavino Heights on 7 September and then the town of Shlissel'burg on 8 September, thereby severing Leningrad's last land link with the outside world. A handful of Soviet naval gunners held out in the nearby Oreshek citadel, located in the mouth of the Neva River. Meanwhile, the rest of XXXIX AK (mot.) turned eastwards towards the Volkhov, where the 54th Army was just beginning to form.

A Czech-made 240mm M16 cannon from II/Artillerie-Regiment 84 shells Leningrad from its position near the Peterhof in October 1941. These were the heaviest artillery pieces available to Heeresgruppe Nord at the start of the siege. (Nik Cornish at Stavka)

The Axis advance upon Leningrad, 20 August–9 November 1941

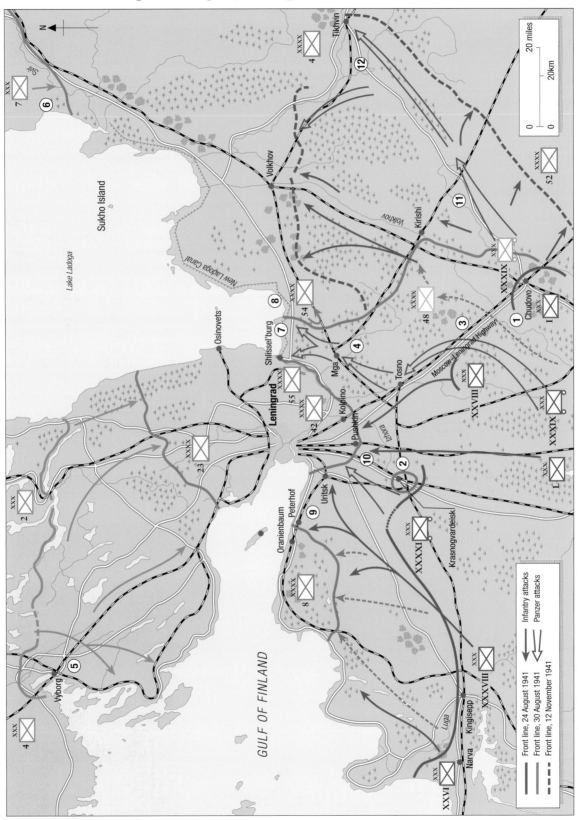

An He 111 bomber dropping a string of eight 200kg bombs. Luftwaffe attacks on Leningrad in the autumn of 1941 inflicted several thousand casualties but were too small scale to accomplish Hitler's goal of 'levelling' the city. (Nik Cornish at Stavka)

Leeb was aware by late August that he would soon have to transfer 4. Panzergruppe and Fliegerkorps VIII to Heeresgruppe Mitte for the up-coming Operation *Typhoon* so he decided to make one last offensive push towards Leningrad with these forces, in the hope of breaking Soviet resistance. However, none of AOK 18 was available since it was still in Estonia, while most of AOK 16 was focused on creating a new front along the Volkhov River. Only Reinhardt's XXXXI AK (mot.) and the infantry from XXVIII and L AK were available for the final attack towards Leningrad.

Hoepner's *Panzergruppe* began its offensive on the morning of 9 September and rapidly enveloped the defenders of Krasnogvardeisk and captured the key Dudergof Heights south of Krasnoye Selo. Soviet militiamen put up a stiff fight for Krasnoye Selo but the town fell on 12 September and German motorized spearheads made a spectacular advance that reached the edge of the Pulkovo Heights by that evening. For the first time, German troops could actually observe Leningrad, some 12km distant. However, the Germans were also within range of the KBF and and they began pounding Reinhardt's spearheads with frequent barrages of large-calibre artillery fire.

Voroshilov committed his last reserves, which failed to stop the German spearheads from reaching the town of Pulkovo, which was held only by militia. Yet the German infantry units advancing on Hoepner's flanks made much slower progress and were gradually stopped by dense Soviet defenses at Uritsk and Kolpino. Rather than weakening, Soviet resistance seemed to grow stronger as the Germans got closer to Leningrad.

In Moscow, the Stavka became concerned when it learned of the fall of Mga and Shlissel'burg and Stalin relieved Voroshilov of command and sent General Georgiy Zhukov to Leningrad to stiffen the city's defences. Zhukov arrived in Leningrad by plane on 13 September and promptly relieved Ivanov of command of the 42nd Army for failing to stop Hoepner's offensive and replaced him with his protégé, General-Major Ivan I. Fediuninskiy – later promoted to general-lieutenant. Zhukov had no desire to be arrested and executed so he slavishly obeyed Stalin's dictum to conduct immediate all-out counterattacks no matter what the cost. On 17 September, Zhukov informed all commanders in the 42nd and 55th armies that anyone who retreated would be shot, as well as their families.

Soviet MiG-3 fighters from 7 IAP flying above the Peter and Paul fortress in Leningrad on 1 August 1941. In fact, most of Leningrad's air defence was provided by older I-153 and I-16 fighters. (RIA Novosti)

Zhukov ordered the weak 8th Army to launch a counterattack into the left flank of XXXXI AK (mot.) and retake Krasnoye Selo, but the German forces finally broke through the 42nd Army and reached the Gulf of Finland near the Peterhof on 16 September. The 8th Army was now isolated in the Oranienbaum bridgehead and its commander refused to attack, since his units were reduced to 30 per cent strength. Zhukov relieved him. Zhukov then turned to Marshal Kulik's 54th Army, which had just received a couple of newly raised rifle divisions and ordered it to attack XXXIX AK (mot.), retake Siniavino and raise the blockade of Leningrad. This was an impossible task for an army that had just begun forming and Kulik's best unit, the 128th Rifle Division, had barely 2,000 troops. Schmidt's corps easily repulsed Kulik's premature offensive. In grandiose style, Zhukov also ordered the newly formed Neva Operational Group (NOG) – which was barely able to defend a 20km long stretch of the Neva River with two weak divisions – to launch a cross-river attack to link up with the 54th Army. Amazingly, the 115th Rifle Division secured a tiny bridgehead across the river at Nevskaya Dubrovka, but was quickly hemmed in by the German 122. Infanterie-Division. Zhukov's counterattacks achieved nothing except squandering the lives of thousands of Soviet troops.

Refusing to accept that his offensive tactics were not working, Zhukov threw Leningrad's remaining reserves into the path of the German advance, with orders to stand or be shot. He scraped together militia, NKVD and various remnants and dispatched them to the Pulkovo sector, but could not prevent the German XXXXI AK (mot.) from taking Pushkin in a final lunge. Zhukov threw in several companies of KV-1 tanks, which attacked the Germans repeatedly around Pushkin, supported by all remaining heavy artillery and the guns of the KBF. Hoepner's tired motorized units had their hands full trying to stop ten KV tanks with only 37mm anti-tank guns and momentarily lost the initiative. Owing to Hoepner's inability to overcome the aggressive Soviet defence around the Pulkovo Observatory, the Germans did not control the best high ground overlooking the city. Zhukov also succeeded on the flanks, where he sent the new 21st NKVD Rifle Division and 6th Naval Infantry Brigade to defend Uritsk against the 58. Infanterie-Division, and the 168th Rifle Division to reinforce the

Soviet troops removing the bodies of five women killed by German artillery fire in Vosstanya Square in front of Moscow Station early in the siege. During the last four months of 1941, German artillery fired over 30,000 rounds into Leningrad, which, in addition to the bombing, killed about 4,000 civilians. (Fonds of the RGKFD, Krasnogorsk)

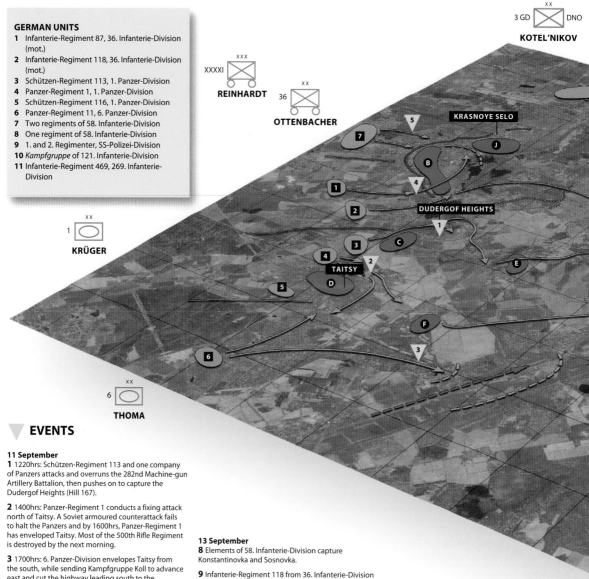

GERMAN UNITS

1 Infanterie-Regiment 87, 36. Infanterie-Division (mot.)
2 Infanterie-Regiment 118, 36. Infanterie-Division (mot.)
3 Schützen-Regiment 113, 1. Panzer-Division
4 Panzer-Regiment 1, 1. Panzer-Division
5 Schützen-Regiment 116, 1. Panzer-Division
6 Panzer-Regiment 11, 6. Panzer-Division
7 Two regiments of 58. Infanterie-Division
8 One regiment of 58. Infanterie-Division
9 1. and 2. Regimenter, SS-Polizei-Division
10 *Kampfgruppe* of 121. Infanterie-Division
11 Infanterie-Regiment 469, 269. Infanterie-Division

3 GD | DNO
KOTEL'NIKOV

XXXXI
REINHARDT

36
OTTENBACHER

KRASNOYE SELO

1
KRÜGER

DUDERGOF HEIGHTS

TAITSY

6
THOMA

▼ EVENTS

11 September

1 1220hrs: Schützen-Regiment 113 and one company of Panzers attacks and overruns the 282nd Machine-gun Artillery Battalion, then pushes on to capture the Dudergof Heights (Hill 167).

2 1400hrs: Panzer-Regiment 1 conducts a fixing attack north of Taitsy. A Soviet armoured counterattack fails to halt the Panzers and by 1600hrs, Panzer-Regiment 1 has enveloped Taitsy. Most of the 500th Rifle Regiment is destroyed by the next morning.

3 1700hrs: 6. Panzer-Division envelopes Taitsy from the south, while sending Kampfgruppe Koll to advance east and cut the highway leading south to the Krasnogvardeisk fortified zone. Koll's artillery shells Soviet troops retreating north on the highway.

4 1800hrs: 36. Infanterie-Division (mot.) attacks the south end of the Krasnoye Selo fortified zone with both regiments, supported by most of the corps artillery and the bulk of Fliegerkorps I and VIII bombers. The attack blasts a hole in the weak defences and the Germans fight their way into the south end of the town.

5 1800hrs: 58. Infanterie-Division conducts a supporting attack against the west side of Krasnoye Selo.

12 September

6 1120hrs: I/Schützen-Regiment 116 advances boldly to Bolshoye Karpino and establishes a hasty defence.

7 1430 hours, 12 September 1941. 36th Infanterie-Division (mot.) captures the rest of Krasnoye Selo, while Infanterie-Regiment 118 drives eastwards against weak resistance.

13 September

8 Elements of 58. Infanterie-Division capture Konstantinovka and Sosnovka.

9 Infanterie-Regiment 118 from 36. Infanterie-Division (mot.) advances north and captures Finskoe Koirovo and the west end of the Pulkovo Heights.

10 1500–1700hrs: A Soviet battalion-sized counterattack with 25 tanks, including three KV-1 and five KV-2s, forces I/Schützen-Regiment 113 to retreat and destroys several PzKpfw III tanks from II/Panzer-Regiment 1. However, a number of the Soviet tanks are immobilized by fire from Panzerjäger-Bataillon 36 and the counterattack collapses.

14–15 September

11 Constant Soviet small counterattacks and naval gunfire pounds the German infantry near the Pulkovo Astronomical Observatory, forcing 36. Infanterie-Division (mot.) troops to dig in.

16 September

12 1. Panzer-Division attacks and captures Aleksandrovka, its last offensive act before beginning to redeploy to Heeresgruppe Mitte.

13 The 121. Infanterie, 269. Infanterie and SS-Polizei-Divisionen advance towards Pushkin from the south, clearing out numerous bunker complexes. Southern Pushkin is captured by 1. Regiment of SS-Polizei-Division.

17 September

14 1200hrs: 2. Regiment of SS-Polizei-Division clears out north Pushkin after heavy fighting. A counterattack by six KV-1 tanks fails and one is destroyed.

XXXXI AK (MOT.) ATTACK, 11–18 SEPTEMBER 1941

Viewed from the south, showing the main German attack toward the outer defences of Leningrad. The Soviet 42nd Army was only able to delay, not stop, the German advance to the gates of Leningrad.

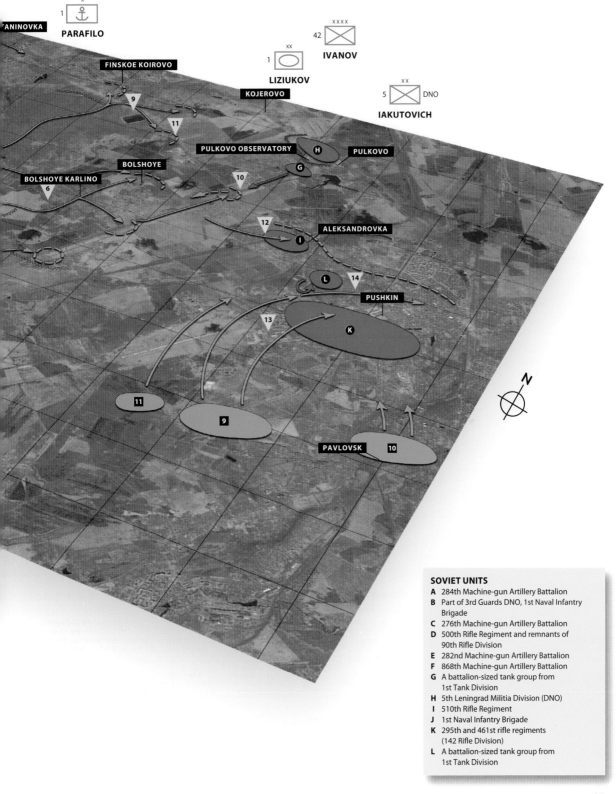

PARAFILO

ANINOVKA

LIZIUKOV

IVANOV

IAKUTOVICH

5 DNO

FINSKOE KOIROVO

KOJEROVO

PULKOVO OBSERVATORY

PULKOVO

BOLSHOYE

BOLSHOYE KARLINO

ALEKSANDROVKA

PUSHKIN

PAVLOVSK

SOVIET UNITS
A 284th Machine-gun Artillery Battalion
B Part of 3rd Guards DNO, 1st Naval Infantry
   Brigade
C 276th Machine-gun Artillery Battalion
D 500th Rifle Regiment and remnants of
   90th Rifle Division
E 282nd Machine-gun Artillery Battalion
F 868th Machine-gun Artillery Battalion
G A battalion-sized tank group from
   1st Tank Division
H 5th Leningrad Militia Division (DNO)
I 510th Rifle Regiment
J 1st Naval Infantry Brigade
K 295th and 461st rifle regiments
   (142 Rifle Division)
L A battalion-sized tank group from
   1st Tank Division

The Soviet battleship *October Revolution* in 1936. She and her sister ship the *Marat* mounted 12 305mm guns in four triple turrets and 16 120mm guns. Although severely battered by Luftwaffe attacks, these two capital ships continued to play a significant role in the defence of Leningrad. (Naval Historical Center, NH71478)

militia at Kolpino. The German 58. Infanterie-Division succeeded in fighting its way into Uritsk – within six kilometres of the Kirov Factory – and captured over 1,000 Soviet troops but was finally stopped by naval infantry, a few KV tanks and concentrated naval gunfire. An even more impressive defensive stand was achieved south of Kolpino, where the 168th Rifle Division and the Izhorsk militia conducted a fanatical defence against the 121. and 122. Infanterie-Divisionen.

After being granted a short extension by the OKH, 4. Panzergruppe began redeploying on 18 September and Leeb ordered his remaining forces to establish siege lines around the city. At a cost of 3,440 casualties between 9 and 16 September, 4. Panzergruppe had advanced to within six to ten kilometres of the southern edge of Leningrad and had captured 25,000 prisoners. Küchler's AOK 18 would conduct siege operations against the Oranienbaum salient and Leningrad, while AOK 16 held the Volkhov. However, desperate Soviet defensive successes at Pulkovo and Kolpino – both of which were objectives that Leeb intended to take – prevented the Germans from getting as close to Leningrad as they intended and left the Soviet command with valuable springboards for future counteroffensives.

Siege operations and the starvation winter

The German encirclement of Leningrad had trapped four armies – the 8th, 23rd, 42nd and 55th – inside the city and the nearby Oranienbaum salient, with a total of 20 divisions and over 300,000 troops. There were also three million civilians trapped in the city. At the beginning of the siege, there were about 30 days' food reserves on hand in the city, but this was further reduced when the Luftwaffe bombed the Badaev food warehouses on 8 September. The Ladoga Flotilla, using barges, could bring in only about 22,000 tons of food per month, when the city needed 30,000 tons. It took 16 hours for a barge convoy to cross the Lake to Osinovets and the Luftwaffe mercilessly attacked them in October–November, sinking 24 of 31 barges and six steamers. A special aviation group with Li 2 transport planes was able to bring in another 600 tons per week. Nor was food the only crippling shortage – fuel was rapidly depleted, which shut down most of the city's electrical power system. As pipes froze from lack of heat, the water system also broke down, which threatened public health and made it harder to fight fires caused

TOP

A company of female volunteers in a workers' battalion formed in Leningrad during 1942. Over 10,000 women were formed into 20 workers' battalions for the internal defence of Leningrad. (Courtesy of Tass)

BOTTOM

Some of Leningrad's improvised defences were more show than substance. A Soviet GAZ-AA truck passes through one of the outer defensive belts of Leningrad, where prefabricated concrete 'dragons' teeth' have been emplaced as anti-tank obstacles. However, these concrete blocks have not been reinforced with steel rods or anchored to the ground, which would have made them fairly simple for combat engineers to remove. (Fonds of the RGKFD, Krasnogorsk)

by German bombardment. By November 1941, Leningrad's civilians began to face real starvation just as winter arrived.

Küchler's AOK 18 conducted the siege with XXVI AK (three divisions) containing the Oranienbaum bridgehead and L AK (four divisions) holding the front from Uritsk to Shlissel'burg. German artillery started shelling Leningrad on 4 September and the Luftwaffe began a month of sustained attacks. Since AOK 18 settled into winter positions early, it managed to avoid the heavy casualties from sickness and frostbite that afflicted Heeresgruppe Mitte in front of Moscow, but the weather did cause significant losses among their horses. As temperatures dropped in early November 1941, AOK 18's horses began dying in droves; for example, after losing only 67 horses during the entire summer campaign, the SS-Polizei-Division lost 1,200 horses during the winter of 1941/42.

The Oreshek citadel (the 'hard little nut'), located where the Neva River enters Lake Ladoga and adjacent to Shlissel'burg. Lenin's older brother was executed here in 1887. In September 1941, only 12 Soviet sailors held the fortress but the Germans passed on the opportunity to storm this vital position while Soviet forces were in disarray.
(Phil Curme Collection)

The winter snow also brought another kind of darkness. SS-Einsatzgruppe A, under SS-Brigadeführer Walter Stahlecker, followed right behind Heeresgruppe Nord and set up headquarters in Krasnogvardeisk in October 1941, not far from AOK 18 headquarters in Siverskaya. In the next two months, SS-Einsatzgruppe A murdered at least 1,389 civilians in Krasnogvardeisk and another 800 in Pushkin. In a clear example of the Wehrmacht's involvement in SS atrocities in the Soviet Union, on 20 December 1941 XXVIII AK requested that SS-Einsatzgruppe A deal with the 240 female occupants of an insane asylum located 20km north of Lyuban – which allegedly posed a 'health risk' to nearby German troops. The SS troops promptly marched in and shot all the patients and staff, which satisfied the local German commander. Quartermaster records from AOK 18 also detail the deportation of 4,300 civilians from Leningrad's suburbs in March 1942, who were sent to Germany as slave labourers. These activities incited the creation of Soviet partisan units in AOK 18's rear areas, although they were not very effective until 1943.

Meanwhile, Zhukov left Leningrad on 6 October, leaving Fediuninskiy in temporary command, but two weeks later he was directed to take command of the 54th Army on the Volkhov in preparation for an effort to break the blockade. General-Lieutenant Mikhail S. Khozin then took over the Leningrad Front. Khozin focused most of his effort on strengthening the defences of the 42nd and 55th armies, whose divisions were reduced to only 2,000–3,000 troops each. By November, the 42nd Army managed to fortify the southern approaches to Leningrad with multiple lines of defence, consisting of trenches, bunkers, 'dragon's teeth' and minefields, as well as a density of 17 anti-tank guns per kilometre. Khozin also improved air defence capabilities against the frequent Luftwaffe raids and acted to improve coordination between the Red Army, the KBF and the VVS. Once the Gulf of Finland and Lake Ladoga froze, Khozin also emplaced troops along the coast, to prevent over-ice attacks. Inside the city, Zhdanov established 79 armed worker battalions, totalling 40,000 troops, to provide internal security in each of the city's districts. Numerous bunkers and obstacles were emplaced throughout the city, in the event of a sudden German breakthrough.

A department store on the Starinevski Prospect under conversion to a fortified gun position in September 1941. Leningrad's internal defences were strengthened with a series of anti-tank barriers, bunkers and hidden gun positions, which would have made a German assault into the city a very costly operation. (Fonds of the RGKFD, Krasnogorsk)

Nor were Leningrad's troops involved only in static defence. The Stavka ordered Khozin to conduct attacks across the Neva River with both the 55th Army and the NOG, as a precursor to link-up efforts with the 54th Army. Khozin continued to feed more troops into the tiny Nevskaya Dubrovka bridgehead, which reduced both the 20th NKVD Rifle Division and 168th Rifle Division to fewer than 300 troops.

Although Khozin and Zhdanov succeeded in hardening Leningrad's defences, they failed to do much to alleviate the effects of the siege on the city's population. The LMC failed to authorize any kind of evacuation before the city was surrounded and once that occurred, Zhdanov put priority on evacuating the Kirov and Bolshevik factories and 10,000 technicians by barge. These efforts succeeded in relocating these vital war industries, but significant civilian evacuation did not begin over the ice road until February 1942. The results were predictable; starvation, lack of heat and typhus ravaged Leningrad's civilian population during the winter of 1941/42, resulting in the deaths of over 600,000 civilians. Even though the troops defending Leningrad received better rations, at least 12,400 also starved to death that winter and another 62,000 were too sick to function. By November, Leningrad's defenders were receiving only 500g of food per day, and by January half of the divisions inside Leningrad were down to 30 per cent strength. Virtually all of the horses were eaten and there was little fuel left for vehicles, so the 42nd and 55th armies quickly lost their mobility. Morale was poor and thousands of Soviet soldiers deserted to the German lines to avoid starvation. Meanwhile, the German troops remained in their siege lines, relatively warm and receiving three times as much food as their opponents, waiting for starvation to win the battle for them.

Eventually, the effects of the siege reduced most of the troops within Leningrad to near combat-ineffectiveness by spring 1942, thereby preventing them from playing even a supporting role in the disastrous Lyuban offensive. Owing to the inactivity on the Leningrad front, Lindemann was able to transfer a number of units from XXVI and L AK to assist with the fighting on the Volkhov, leaving the siege lines very thinly held.

The Tikhvin gambit

As the fighting around Leningrad began to ebb in mid-October 1941, both sides considered their options. With most of its armour and air support gone, Heeresgruppe Nord lacked the strength to break into the city but the emaciated Soviet 42nd and 55th armies lacked the strength to break out. A period of attritional stalemate, reminiscent of the Western Front in World War I, settled over the front as the first snow fell on Leningrad on 14 October. Both sides received modest reinforcements: Leeb received five *Fallschirmjäger* battalions from 7. Flieger-Division to augment the flimsy defences on the Neva River, while Fediuninskiy's 54th Army on the Volkhov received the half-strength 3rd and 4th guards rifle divisions.

The Stavka insisted on breaking the blockade as soon as possible, which meant another pincer attack on Siniavino from the 54th Army and the NOG. Meanwhile, the OKH sought measures to accelerate Leningrad's strangulation and it believed that Heeresgruppe Nord still had the strength to advance east and capture Volkhov and Tikhvin, thereby severing the rail lines that supported the Lake Ladoga barge traffic. Leeb opted to commit his last mobile strike force – four divisions of XXXIX AK (mot.) and three infantry divisions of I AK – to penetrate the seam between the Soviet 4th and 52nd armies near Chudovo and advance north-eastwards to capture Tikhvin.

The German offensive began on 16 October and after four days of fighting, achieved a major breakthrough. Despite awful terrain, poor weather and 30cm of snow on the ground, 12. Panzer-Division was able to advance over 60km within 12 days and Tikhvin was finally captured on 8 November. Without this rail junction, the food situation in the city became critical. However, the seven German divisions involved in the offensive had suffered 10,032 casualties in a month. Both men and vehicles were spent and the German logistic system couldn't get adequate food, fuel or ammunition through the icy trails to Tikhvin. Generalleutnant von Arnim took command at Tikhvin and gathered his available forces into a hedgehog defence of the town and hoped that the Soviets were too weak to take advantage of the German predicament.

Meretskov was brought in to take command of the 4th Army and to orchestrate the 52nd and 54th armies for an immediate counterattack. The Stavka gave Meretskov three full-strength divisions from the Trans-Baikal and Far East military districts.

Meretskov began a concentric attack upon the German hedgehog in Tikhvin on 12 November, while the 54th Army attacked the German I AK on the northern side of the salient and the 52nd Army attacked XXXVIII AK on the south side. Meretskov's offensive gradually drove in both German flanks and elements of the 126. and 254. Infanterie-Divisionen were surrounded. German supply lines to Tikhvin collapsed and Arnim had to resort to emergency air re-supply of ammunition.

With the German flanks crumbling, Meretskov launched an all-out attack on Tikhvin on 4 December and four days later Arnim abandoned the town. Falling back to the Volkhov, the ten German divisions established a new front by the end of December. However, these ten divisions had suffered a total of 21,530 casualties, including 4,600 dead. Furthermore, both 8. and 12. Panzer-Divisionen were burnt out, leaving Heeresgruppe Nord with no mobile reserves. After the successful recapture of Tikhvin, the Stavka reorganized the Soviet forces in this area and created the Volkhov Front under Meretskov's command.

Air–sea operations around Leningrad, 1941/42

At the start of the war, the Voyenno-Vozdushnye Sily (VVS) had seven fighter and six bomber regiments based near Leningrad, with a total of 426 fighters and 182 medium bombers. Nearly three-quarters of the fighters were obsolete I-153s and I-16s, but the 7th and 159th Fighter Regiments had recently been equipped with the new MiG-3 fighter. While the primary mission of the VVS was battlefield support, General-Major F. Kryukov's PVO forces were responsible for the air defence of Leningrad itself. The 7th Fighter Corps, still forming at the start of the war, had eight fighter regiments with 312 I-153 and I-16 fighters. Leningrad's inner air defence relied on the PVO's 2nd Air Defence Corps, which had six flak regiments (about 300 76mm and 85mm guns), 230 machine guns, 300 searchlights, 360 barrage balloons and 302 observation posts. However unlike London in 1940, the Soviets had only a single experimental RUS-2 air warning radar at Toksovo, north-east of Leningrad. Instead, the VVS/PVO was dependent upon ground observers and flying standing patrols over the city and the Lake Ladoga supply lines – which resulted in high rates of attrition. In addition, the KBF had another three fighter regiments with 180 I-15bis and I-16 fighters assigned to defend the fleet and a flak regiment with 68 guns to defend Kronstadt.

The Luftwaffe first appeared near Leningrad before dawn on 22 June 1941, when 18 Ju 88 bombers flew into Soviet airspace and dropped 36 1,000kg magnetic mines in the sea channel off Kronstadt. The dumbfounded Soviet anti-aircraft gunners watched the spectacle but held their fire, since war was not yet official. Afterwards, the Luftwaffe continued to mine the waters around Kronstadt and Leningrad, as well as bombing the New Ladoga Canal to interdict barge traffic into the city. As Heeresgruppe Nord approached Leningrad, Luftwaffe bombers launched a number of precision attacks on major railroad bridges leading into the city to interdict reinforcements.

By late August 1941, Generaloberst Alfred Keller's Luftflotte I still possessed about 100 fighters and 200 bombers, while the VVS-North-western Front under General-Major Aleksandr Novikov had lost much of its strength in trying to slow the German advance. Furthermore, Generaloberst Wolfram von Richthofen's Fliegerkorps VIII, with its four Stuka groups and Bf 110 fighters, arrived to reinforce the final stage of the German advance on

German *Fallschirmjäger* manning a Pak 36 37mm anti-tank gun near Leningrad in November 1941. The 7. Flieger-Division rushed in five battalions to hold the Neva River line near Marino and suffered over 2,700 casualties in just six weeks of defensive combat. (Nik Cornish at Stavka)

The Germans concentrated their remaining mobile forces to seize and hold Tikhvin but they could not logistically sustain a motorized corps at this distance from their railheads. This PzKpfw III was one of the few tanks that remained operational by December 1941. (HITM Archives, 06110361)

Leningrad. In mid-September, Luftflotte I and the VVS-North-western Front fought desperately to gain air superiority over the battlefield and the three fighter Gruppen of Major Johannes Trautloft's JG 54 'Grünherz' (Green Hearts) wreaked havoc on Novikov's forces. To redress the imbalance, the Stavka dispatched five more fighter regiments, as well as 90 of the new LaGG-3 fighters and 100 IL-2 Sturmoviks, to reinforce Novikov's command. Nevertheless, JG 54's fighter sweeps managed to shoot down 39 of the 55 LaGG-3s assigned to the 7th IAK/PVO in September 1941 and the air-to-air kill ratio was about six: one in the Luftwaffe's favour. By the end of the month, the 7th IAK/PVO had lost 80 per cent of its pilots.

While each side's fighters fought for air superiority, the bombers were sent in to soften up the enemy. Leningrad experienced its first major air raid on the night of 8/9 September when 27 Ju 88 bombers struck the city with incendiary bombs. The heaviest raids occurred on 17 and 19 September. In all, Luftflotte I flew 675 night bombing sorties over Leningrad in September, which inflicted 4,400 casualties. The PVO air defence units eventually succeeded in discouraging daylight raids over Leningrad but they were unable to counter night bomber raids effectively. In desperation, the VVS adopted 'taran' (ramming) attacks. Over 20 'taran' attacks were conducted in the Leningrad area in September and they made a big impression on the Luftwaffe bomber pilots. Furthermore, Novikov used some of his new Il-2 Sturmoviks to mount raids on the nearby German airfields with some successes, destroying seven Ju 88 bombers on the ground at Siverskaya on 7 November.

In addition to supporting the ground battle and 'levelling' Leningrad, Keller was also tasked with neutralizing the KBF. Fliegerkorps VIII made a major raid on Kronstadt on 23 September that detonated the forward magazine on the battleship *Marat*, damaged the battleship *October Revolution* and sank the destroyers *Minsk* and *Steregushchiy*. However, Soviet fighter and flak opposition over Kronstadt was intense and the raid cost Fliegerkorps VIII six aircraft. The attack on Kronstadt proved to be the swan song for Luftflotte I's aerial offensive, since Fliegerkorps VIII was transferred south to support Operation *Typhoon*. Thereafter, Keller focused his remaining forces on maintaining air superiority over critical battlefield areas and providing close air support to AOK 18.

Heavy aerial combat continued around Leningrad throughout autumn 1941, but both sides were essentially fought out by the fall of Tikhvin. After a loss of over 2,700 aircraft since the start of the war, the VVS-Northwestern Front was reduced to fewer than 200 operational aircraft and most of its trained aircrew were gone. Luftflotte I had lost about 300 aircraft, including 70 fighters and 162 bombers and KG 76 and KG 77 were sent home to rebuild, leaving fewer than 150 operational aircraft on the Leningrad front. While JG 54 claimed over 1,100 'kills' by this point, it had but 30 operational Bf 109Fs left to contest the skies around Leningrad. Keller was less willing to risk his few remaining bombers against flak and 'taran' attacks over Leningrad merely to kill civilians, so he reduced bomber raids to small attacks involving a few aircraft. Operations against the 'ice road' on Lake Ladoga were also limited by poor weather and lack of ground attack aircraft. Meanwhile, Novikov spent the winter rebuilding his shattered fighter units with new LaGG-3, Hurricane and P-40 fighters. He also took control over the PVO forces in the city, which led to better coordination between fighters, anti-aircraft guns and early warning assets. Just before the Gulf of Finland froze over, most of the KBF moved in to moorings along the Neva River, tucked in tight next to the anti-aircraft batteries.

Although the Soviet surface warships were virtually immobilized, the KBF hoped to use its large submarine force – which numbered 64 boats at the start of the siege – to harass German merchant traffic in the Baltic. However, the Germans quickly established an effective mine and ASW barrier around Kronstadt in the autumn of 1941, which made it increasingly hazardous for Soviet submarines to break out into the Gulf of Finland. The KBF dispatched 21 submarines from Kronstadt in the autumn of 1941, losing ten boats and accomplishing very little. Submarine operations then ceased for the winter once Kronstadt was iced in.

By January 1942, Luftflotte I had only 89 operational combat aircraft against 230 Soviet aircraft. The Stavka managed to ship in ten RUS-2 radars to Leningrad to help boost early warning, although the network was not fully operational until mid-1942. Despite improved air defence capabilities, the

The destroyer *Opytny* (*Skilful*), hidden in the Neva River, conducts a night bombardment with its three 130mm guns on 1 January 1942. The *Opytny* was one of the few destroyers in the KBF to survive the war intact. (RIA Novosti, 59990)

A convoy of Soviet trucks crossing the ice road over Lake Ladoga in February or March 1942. The air cover overhead was unusual in the winter of 1941/42 and the Soviets built numerous anti-aircraft batteries on the ice to protect the road from attack. Without this lifeline, Leningrad would not have survived the winter. (Fonds of the RGKFD, Krasnogorsk)

VVS had limited offensive capabilities owing to its heavy losses in bombers in 1941. Keller also provided many close support sorties against the 2nd Shock Army and interdiction sorties against its railhead at Malaya Vishera, but low-level missions resulted in significant bomber losses to flak. Between February and April 1942, Luftflotte I lost 41 bombers, 21 Stukas and 19 fighters, while claiming 581 Soviet aircraft destroyed. Once the 2nd Shock Army was encircled, Luftflotte I played a major role in its destruction. When the Soviets tried to conduct aerial resupply missions at night to Vlasov's trapped forces, Keller pressed JG 54 into service as night fighters and they succeeded in shooting down over 30 transports over the pocket, which crippled Soviet resupply efforts. Meanwhile, bombers from KG 3 and KG 53 mercilessly plastered Vlasov's troops from the air, inflicting great losses.

When the spring thaw came, Keller was ordered to make another attempt to smash the KBF. Luftflotte I was reinforced with two Stuka groups armed with 1,000kg armour-piercing bombs. However, a dense ring of anti-aircraft guns now protected the KBF. The first attack, Operation *Eisstoß* (ice assault), was conducted on 4 April 1942 by 62 Stukas, 70 bombers and 59 Bf-109s, but heavy AA fire severely disrupted German bombing accuracy. The raid achieved seven hits on the heavy cruiser *Maxim Gorky*, four hits on the battleship *October Revolution* and minor damage to eleven other warships, but no ships were sunk. On 20 April, Luftflotte I resumed its attack on the KBF with Operation *Götz von Berlichingen*, but again the dense AA defences limited damage to several destroyers and support ships. Recognizing its inability to sink the KBF, Luftflotte I stepped up its mining operations in the Gulf of Finland but made no further efforts against the KBF for the rest of the siege.

For the first and only time during the siege, Luftflotte I made a major effort to disrupt Soviet logistics over Lake Ladoga in late May 1942. On 28 May, 80 aircraft bombed the ports of Kobona and Lednyovo on the eastern side of the lake, inflicting minor damage. The next day, another major raid struck Osinevets on the western side. Soviet fighter interception, cued by the new radars, succeeded in shooting down three German aircraft in these raids. After that, Keller sent most of his bombers to support the fighting on the Volkhov Front, but dispatched a single Staffel of 15 Bf 109s from JG 54 to the Finnish airbase of Petäjärvi to interdict barge traffic on Lake Ladoga, but in 104 sorties it failed to sink a single ship.

In June 1942, the Axis made a rare joint effort to establish a naval task force on Lake Ladoga, known as Naval Detachment K. Four Italian MAS torpedo boats and four small German minelayers were trucked in to form the initial detachment, which operated from the Finnish-held side of the lake. Thirty Siebel ferries, armed with artillery pieces and flak guns, soon arrived to bolster this force. On 22 October 1942, Detachment K conducted Operation *Brazil*, a major raid against Suho Island on the south side of the lake. The Axis forces succeeded in knocking out the Soviet coastal battery on the island, but were forced to beat a hasty retreat when Soviet aircraft and motor torpedo boats counterattacked. Four Siebel ferries were lost and the Germans suffered 79 casualties. Chastised by their defeat, the Axis disbanded Naval Detachment K and attempted no further naval operations on Lake Ladoga.

LENINGRAD ENCIRCLED, 1942

Meretskov's success at Tikhvin now worked against him, as it gave Stalin an unrealistic appraisal of the Volkhov Front's offensive capabilities. Soviet

The German Eisenbahn-Artillerie-Batterie 686 arrived on the Leningrad front in the winter of 1941/42 equipped with two captured French 520mm M18 L/16 mortars to shell Leningrad. However, in March 1942 it was re-equipped with two French 400mm 752(f) howitzers. Located near the Peterhof, this was the heaviest artillery actually used by the Germans in the siege. (Author's collection)

The Lyuban Offensive, 4–30 January 1942

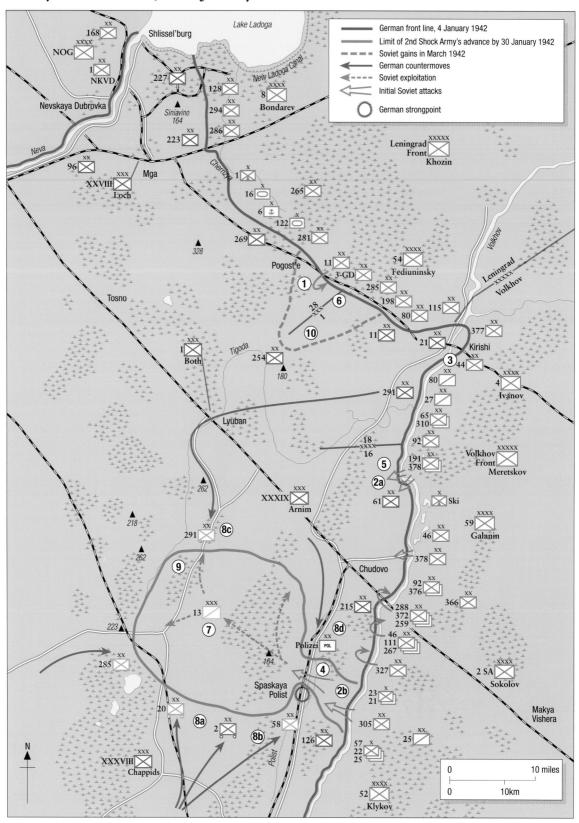

Legend:
- German front line, 4 January 1942
- Limit of 2nd Shock Army's advance by 30 January 1942
- Soviet gains in March 1942
- German countermoves
- Soviet exploitation
- Initial Soviet attacks
- German strongpoint

Lake Ladoga

Shlissel'burg

New Ladoga Canal

168 · NOG · 1 NKVD · 227 · 128 · 8 Bondarev · 294 · 286 · 223

Nevskaya Dubrovka · Siniavino 164 · Chernaya

96 · XXVIII Loch · Mga · 1 · 16 · 6 · 122 · 265 · 281 · 269

328

Tosno · Pogost'e · 11 3-GD · 54 Fediuninsky · 285 · 198 · 80 · 115 · Leningrad Front Khozin · Leningrad Volkhov · Volkhov

① · 28 1 · ⑥ · ⑩ · 11 · 21 · 377 · Kirishi · ③ · 44 · 4 Ivanov

I Both · Tigoda · 254 · 180 · 291 · 80 · 27 · 65 310 · 92 · 191 378 · Volkhov Front Meretskov

Lyuban · 262 · 18 16 · ⑤ · ②a · 61 · Ski · 59 Galanin

218 · 262 · XXXIX Arnim · 46 · 378

291 · ⑧c · ⑨ · Chudovo · 92 376 · 366

13 · ⑦ · 164 · 215 · 288 372 259 · 46 111 267 · 327 · 2 SA Sokolov

223 · 285 · Polizei POL · ⑧d · ④ · 23 21 · Makya Vishera

20 · ⑧a · 2 · ⑧b · 58 · ② b · 305 · 25

Spaskaya Polist · 126 · 57 22 25

N

XXXVIII Chappids · Polist · 52 Klykov

0 ———— 10 miles
0 ———— 10km

1 4 January: The Soviet 54th Army attacks the seam of I and XXVIII AK near Pogost'e with two divisions, but is easily repulsed by a German counterattack.

2 6 January: Galanin's 59th Army attacks on a wide front both north and south of Chudovo, but gains only two small bridgeheads across the Volkhov:

a Two ski battalions succeed in gaining a toehold in the 61. Infanterie-Division sector.

b The 305th Rifle Division and several brigades of the 2nd Shock Army cross the Volkhov near the seam of the 126. and the 215. Infanterie-Divisionen.

3 6 January: Ivanov's 4th Army fails to cross Volkhov south of Kirishi. Although it tried again on 13 January, 4th Army failed to close a pincer around the German I AK.

4 7 January: the 305th Rifle Division and brigades of 2nd Shock Army succeed in creating a small hole in the security zone of the 126. Infanterie-Division, but cannot penetrate the main line of resistance.

5 13–17 January: Meretskov reinforces the small 59th Army bridgehead and renews the offensive. After four days, a small breakthrough is achieved and 2nd Shock Army's spearheads advance ten kilometres.

6 13–17 January: Fediuninsky's 54th Army renews attack near Pogost'e and succeeds in capturing the town, but is stopped by German reinforcements.

7 21–24 January: The 2nd Shock Army continues to fight its way through the German defences but cannot capture the strongpoints at Spasskaya Polist. Meretskov commits the 13th Cavalry Corps into the breach to exploit.

8 25–30 January: Küchler and Lindemann rush forces to the area to seal off the Soviet breakthrough:

a 285. Sicherungs-Division, a *Kampfgruppe* from 20. Infanterie-Division (mot.) and 2. SS-Infanterie-Brigade (mot.) form blocking positions on the southern side of the penetration.

b The 58. Infanterie-Division arrives to counterattack the southern side of the penetration.

c Elements of the 291. Infanterie-Division are transferred from Kirishi to defend the southern approaches to Lyuban.

d The SS-Polizei-Division arrives to counterattack the northern side of the penetration.

9 Line reached by 2nd Shock Army spearheads by end of January 1942.

10 9–20 March: Fediuninsky's 54th Army resumes the attack near Pogost'e in March and achieves a substantial penetration before stopped by German reserves.

troops had barely reached their new positions along the Volkhov River when Stalin demanded that Meretskov launch a major offensive in less than two weeks with the grand objective of penetrating AOK 16's front between Kirishi and Novgorod and then advancing over 100km to capture Siverskaya, thus raising the siege of Leningrad. A large number of Siberian reserve divisions and rifle brigades raised in the Volga Military District began to arrive on the Volkhov Front in mid-December, providing Meretskov, on paper, with four armies totalling 32 divisions. In reality, Meretskov's units were desperately short of artillery, fuel and ammunition to mount a proper set-piece offensive against a dug-in enemy over difficult terrain. Furthermore, Stalin – fearful of concentrating too much power under one general – ordered that the northern part of the relief effort, the 8th and 54th armies, remain under the control of Khozin's Leningrad Front.

After retiring from Tikhvin, the Germans established a thinly held front along the Volkhov. Küchler's AOK 18 held the Siniavino–Mga corridor with XXVIII AK, while I and XXXIX AK (mot.) held the Kirishi salient. Busch's AOK 16 held the Volkhov between Chudovo and Novgorod with its XXXVIII AK. Heeresgruppe Nord had negligible reserves.

A German MG34 machine-gun position located on the edge of a village on the Volkhov front during the winter of 1941/42. Note that this position has little cover from enemy mortar fire but does have a fairly open engagement area out to the wood line. (HITM Archives)

Meretskov planned to use the new 59th Army under General-Major Ivan Galanin to penetrate the German XXXVIII AK's front south of Chudovo near Spasskaya Polist and, once a breakthrough was achieved, to pass the 2nd Shock Army through to exploit into the German rear and drive on Lyuban. The 2nd Shock Army, under the command of General-Lieutenant Grigorii Sokolov, was a new formation composed of one rifle division, eight rifle brigades, six ski battalions and two tank battalions, a total of about 50,000 troops. Meanwhile, the Soviet 4th (Ivanov) and 54th (Fediuninskiy) armies would attack the Kirishi salient from both sides in order to encircle the German I AK. On the flanks, the 8th Army (Bondarev) would attack near Mga and the 52nd Army (Klykov) would attack towards Novgorod, merely to prevent Küchler from transferring forces from these sectors. As usual at this phase of the war, the Soviets attempted to do far too much with multiple, poorly coordinated and under-resourced attacks. Meretskov realized that the mission was overly ambitious but he had no desire to go back to an NKVD prison so he dutifully carried out preparations for the offensive to begin in early January.

Fediuninskiy's 54th Army kicked off the offensive on 4 January 1942 with an attack on the German I AK at Pogost'e, west of Kirishi, but failed miserably. Two days later, the main Volkhov offensive began with multiple attacks by the 4th, 52nd and 59th armies, but these initial attacks were a near-complete failure across the entire front. Galanin's 59th Army had plenty of infantry – 60 battalions – but only 24 multiple rocket launchers and most of his tube artillery consisted of lightweight 76mm guns instead of 122mm or 152mm howitzers. Air support was negligible. Nevertheless, Galanin's infantrymen gained a small bridgehead across the Volkhov River and by massing 15 rifle battalions against three German battalions of Infanterie-Regiment 426, succeeded in tearing a small hole in 126. Infanterie-Division's forward defences. Under pressure from the Stavka to make a breakthrough, Meretskov committed the 2nd Shock Army into this 'breach' on 7 January. Charging into this narrow salient, Sokolov's shock troops suffered 3,000 casualties and after two days of fruitless fighting, the offensive fell apart. The Stavka ordered a temporary halt to the entire offensive, replaced Sokolov with General-Lieutenant Nikolai Klykov from 52nd Army and ordered Meretskov to renew the offensive as soon as his forces were reorganized.

A Soviet 85mm anti-aircraft battery, located on Vasilevsky Island, inside besieged Leningrad in February 1942. The former St Isaac's Cathedral is in the background. Amazingly, a prominent target like St Isaac's suffered no direct hits during the entire siege. (RIA Novosti Photo)

Meretskov used the brief interlude to bring up more heavy artillery and he decided to make greater use of his 18 ski battalions, which had not been ready at the start of the offensive. The 59th and 2nd Shock armies renewed their attacks south of Spasskaya Polist on 13 January and after four days of costly fighting, succeeded in making a small penetration between the German 126. and 215. Infanterie-Divisionen at Myasnoy Bor. Fediuninskiy's 54th Army also succeeded in capturing Pogost'e and made a dent in I AK's defences, as well as inflicting over 1,300 casualties. However, the Soviets received a rude shock when they found that their KV-1 and T-34 tanks were no longer immune to German anti-tank fire. Sturmgeschütz-Batterie 667 had just received a shipment of Gr. 38 HEAT rounds and between 18 and 20 January, two of its StuG III assault guns used the HEAT ammunition to destroy four KV-1s and five T-34s near Pogost'e. On the flanks, attacks by the Soviet 8th, 4th and 52nd armies made no gains, but the Spanish 250. Infanterie-Division received a harsh baptism of fire. Most of the Soviet attacks had been repulsed, but Leeb's nerves were frayed after months of attritional combat and he mentioned withdrawal from the Volkhov. Instead, Hitler relieved Leeb of command of Heeresgruppe Nord and replaced him with Generaloberst Georg Küchler. There would be no more retreats – Heeresgruppe Nord would stand and fight on the Volkhov.

Between 17 and 23 January, the 59th and 2nd Shock armies kept pounding away at Myasnoy Bor, making small gains. The two German divisions holding the shoulders of the breach – the 126. and 215. Infanterie-Divisionen – were badly hurt themselves, with over 1,200 casualties. Küchler tried to block the Soviet penetration with any forces at hand, including the newly arrived SS-Legion 'Flandern', construction units and police battalions. Since this part of the front was the only area where his forces had achieved any success, Meretskov kept pushing all reserves to this sector to keep the attack going. Normally, a commander's main responsibility in a penetration attack is to widen the shoulders of the breach to enable a real exploitation, but the Soviet troops were unable to eliminate the main German fortified positions at Spasskaya Polist and Zemitsy, and instead the 2nd Shock Army squeezed westwards through a narrow gap between the two German strongpoints. Bowing to pressure from the Stavka, Meretskov committed the

END OF THE FIVE-KOPECK BRIDGEHEAD, 29 APRIL 1942 (pp. 50–51)

Once the blockade of Leningrad began, Zhukov ordered the defenders to establish a bridgehead over the Neva River as a jumping-off point to link up with the expected relief forces from the Volkhov Front. On the evening of 19/20 September 1941, several rifle battalions managed to cross the Neva River on rafts near the town of Dubrovka and establish a small bridgehead, but German troops quickly arrived in force to hem them in. The tiny foothold was dubbed the 'five-kopeck bridgehead' since it was 1,400m wide and extended only 500m from the water's edge; this barren patch of mud had no trees, buildings or any kind of cover. German forces brought the bridgehead under constant artillery and machine-gun fire from three sides; during daylight hours, Soviet troops within the bridgehead could not walk upright and could only crawl. Instead, the soldiers dug fighting positions in the muddy clay of the riverbank. The Leningrad Front kept sending more troops and a few tanks across each night, but the life expectancy of soldiers within the bridgehead averaged only three days. One wounded soldier who was fortunate enough to be evacuated from the bridgehead was Sergeant Vladimir Putin, father of the future Russian president. However when the ice began to break on the Neva in the spring of 1942, the 1,400 soldiers of the 330th Rifle Regiment, 86th Rifle Division, defending the Nevskaya Dubrovka (Nevsky Pyatachok) bridgehead became temporarily isolated. The Germans moved immediately to eliminate this thorn in their side.

At 2020hrs on 24 April, five German infantry assault groups from I/Infanterie-Regiment 43 and 6. Kompagnie of II/Infanterie-Regiment 1 (1. Infanterie-Division) led by Oberst Louis von Pröck attacked and overwhelmed the 2nd Company of the 330th Rifle Regiment in close combat, pushing a bulge into the bridgehead. The remainder of the 330th launched six desperate counterattacks on 25/26 April but failed to drive back the Germans and suffered heavy losses in the process. Soviet artillery support was minimal owing to ammunition shortages. An effort to get some KV-1 heavy tanks (1) across the ice-clogged river resulted in disaster. At 1040hrs on 27 April, the Germans hit both the north and south ends of the bridgehead with the I and II/Infanterie-Regiment 1, supported by Pionier-Bataillon 1 and Artillerie-Regiment 1, quickly overrunning two-thirds of the bridgehead. Most of the surviving Soviet troops were wounded and running out of ammunition. This scene depicts a German assault group (2) attacking the command post of the 330th Rifle Regiment (3) by the water's edge, where the last defenders held out until 2100hrs. At the very end, Soviet soldiers ran out of ammunition and fought back with shovels, bayonets and rocks, until they were snuffed out in a volley of grenades. A few, such as Major Alexander Sokolov, succeeded in swimming back to friendly lines, but the Germans captured 117 prisoners in the bridgehead and the rest of the regiment was dead. The Leningrad Front held the bridgehead for 222 days at a cost of about 30,000 dead, but the German success was temporary since Soviet forces crossed the Neva again on 26 August 1942.

13th Cavalry Corps to follow the 2nd Shock Army into the gap and exploit towards Lyuban. In short order, over 40,000 Soviet troops managed to get behind the German main line of resistance, with the spearheads advanced up to 75km into the rear areas.

This was a moment of crisis for Heeresgruppe Nord, particularly since the penetration occurred near the boundary of AOK 16 and 18 (now under Lindemann). Although the Soviet 2nd Shock Army was bloodied, little stood between it and Lindemann's headquarters in Siverskaya. However, Hitler had found the right man in Küchler. He immediately ordered AOK 18 to contain the northern half of the Soviet penetration by taking units from the Kirishi salient, while AOK 16 contained the southern half with its XXXVIII AK. Owing to the failure of the Soviet 4th Army's attack on Kirishi, I AK was able to transfer part of the 291. Infanterie-Division to block the southern approaches to Lyuban. Simultaneously, Küchler scraped together a blocking force from 285. Sicherungs-Division, 2. SS-Brigade (mot.) and a *Kampfgruppe* from 20. Infanterie-Division (mot.) to hold the western and southern ends of the bulge. Since the Leningrad front was quiet, Küchler was able to thin his siege lines and detach both the 58. Infanterie-Division and SS-Polizei-Division to move south by rail to the Volkhov. He ordered his staff to begin planning a pincer attack known as *Raubtier* (beast of prey), using these two divisions, to cut off the narrow base of the salient. If the Germans kept their heads, there was an opportunity to deal a devastating counterblow to the Volkhov Front.

Given time, Meretskov was capable of achieving a real breakthrough. He organized a special shock group that captured two German strongpoints south of Spasskaya Polist on 12 February, widening the breach to 14km. The German 215. Infanterie-Division was on the verge of collapse, having suffered another 1,448 casualties. Meretskov immediately reinforced the 2nd Shock Army to the equivalent of 15 divisions and its spearheads were well into the German rear areas. Adding to the deteriorating German situation, Fediuninskiy launched a new attack on 15 March at Pogost'e that punched a hole through the 269. Infanterie-Division's defences and succeeded in advancing 22km towards Lyuban. For a brief moment, the two pincers of 2nd Shock Army and 54th Army were only about 35km apart, threatening to encircle eight German divisions. Even worse, the Soviet North-west Front launched a major offensive against AOK 16 south of Lake Il'men and succeeded in encircling 96,000 troops at Demyansk on 8 February and another 5,000 at Kholm. Heeresgruppe Nord was on the verge of a catastrophic defeat.

LEFT
The Soviet heavy cruiser *Maxim Gorky* was damaged by mines, bombing and artillery fire in 1941 and managed to remain afloat only by sheltering within Leningrad's commercial harbour under the protection of barrage balloons and flak batteries. In April 1942, the Luftwaffe scored eight more hits on the cruiser but the Soviets managed to repair her and she provided naval gunfire support during the final breakout in January 1944. (Naval Historical Center, NH95522)

RIGHT
German medics evacuate a casualty on the Volkhov front, spring 1942. Casualty evacuation – even in summer weather – was extremely difficult owing to the lack of roads and the swampy terrain. (Nik Cornish at Stavka)

The destruction of 2nd Shock Army

With victory tantalizingly within Meretskov's grasp, Küchler launched Operation *Raubtier* on the morning of 15 March. The 58. Infanterie-Division and SS-Polizei-Division, supported by Stukas from Luftflotte I, struck the narrow base of the Soviet penetration near Myasnoy Bor. On 20 March, the German pincers met, severing the corridor and trapping over 50,000 Soviet troops of the 2nd Shock Army and 59th Army. Meretskov was able to reopen a tenuous two-kilometre-wide corridor to the trapped units on 27 March, but it was now obvious that Leningrad's rescue force itself needed rescue. The situation rapidly deteriorated as the thaw began in April, accompanied by heavy rains, which melted the ice on the frozen swamps and left much of the territory occupied by the trapped 2nd Shock Army virtually underwater. Meretskov ordered the entire Volkhov Front to shift to the defensive and for his efforts, the Stavka relieved Meretskov on 23 April. In a ridiculous decision, Stalin ordered Khozin – in charge of the Leningrad Front – to also take over the Volkhov Front and rescue the 2nd Shock Army.

On 20 April, General-Lieutenant Andrei Vlasov was flown into the pocket to take charge of the battered 2nd Shock Army. By the time he arrived, most units had been reduced to 30 per cent strength and ammunition and food supplies were virtually exhausted. At first, the Germans were content to pound the trapped Soviet army with artillery fire and to let starvation do the rest. However, Khozin succeeded in organizing several relief attacks that enabled a number of troops to escape the pocket, albeit without their heavy equipment. Concerned that significant numbers of Soviets were escaping, Küchler ordered Lindemann – now responsible for the whole pocket battle – to finish off the 2nd Shock Army. On 30 May, the German I and XXXVIII AK attacked and sealed off the Soviet escape route once and for all. After a desperate breakout attempt failed on 5 June, the 2nd Shock Army fell apart. German infantry then methodically hunted down and destroyed isolated units, piece by piece. Altogether, about 30,000 Soviet troops escaped the pocket before the end, but the Germans took over 32,000 prisoners. By 25 June, Vlasov himself was captured and the pocket was eliminated, although mopping up of stragglers in the swamps continued for weeks afterwards.

Stalin angrily relieved Khozin of command and brought Meretskov back to reorganize the Volkhov Front. Govorov was sent to command the Leningrad Front. Vlasov was made the convenient scapegoat for the entire disaster. From the beginning of the Lyuban Offensive on 7 January 1942 to

Operation *Nordlicht*, 31 August 1942

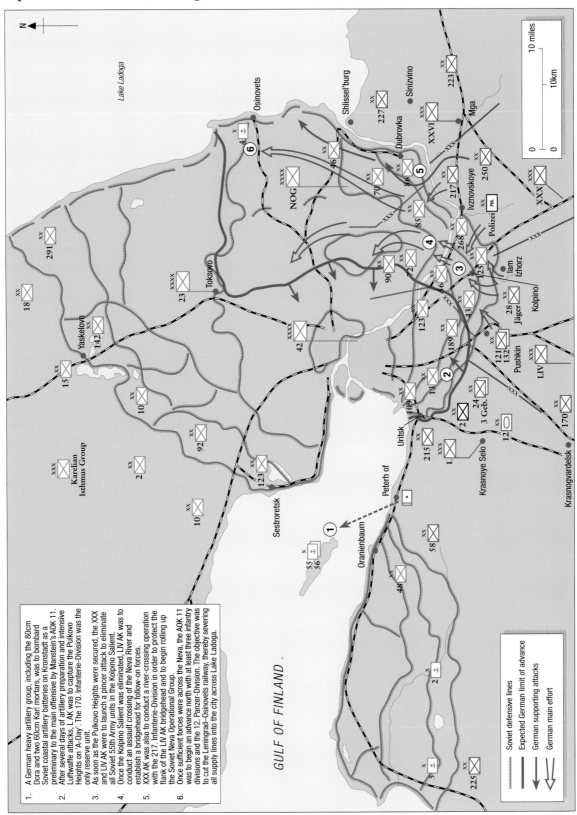

1. A German heavy artillery group, including the 80cm Dora and two 60cm Karl mortars, was to bombard Soviet coastal artillery batteries on Kronstadt as a preliminary to the main offensive by Manstein's AOK 11.
2. After several days of artillery preparation and intensive Luftwaffe attacks, I AK was to capture the Pulkovo Heights on 'A-Day'. The 170. Infanterie-Division was the only reserve unit.
3. As soon as the Pulkovo Heights were secured, the XXX and LIV AK were to launch a pincer attack to eliminate all Soviet 55th Army units in the Kolpino Salient.
4. Once the Kolpino Salient was eliminated, LIV AK was to conduct an assault crossing of the Neva River and establish a bridgehead for follow-on forces.
5. XXX AK was also to conduct a river-crossing operation with the 217. Infanterie-Division in order to protect the flank of the LIV AK bridgehead and to begin rolling up the Soviet Neva Operational Group.
6. Once sufficient forces were across the Neva, the AOK 11 was to begin an advance north with at least three infantry divisions and the 12. Panzer-Division. The objective was to cut the Leningrad–Osinovets railway, thereby severing all supply lines into the city across Lake Ladoga.

Soviet defensive lines

Expected German limit of advance

German supporting attacks

German main effort

General-Lieutenant Andrei A. Vlasov (1900–46), shortly after his capture on 12 July 1942. Although one of the better Soviet commanders of 1941/42, Vlasov feared that he would be arrested after the destruction of his 2nd Shock Army and opted to remain in the Volkhov pocket. As a prisoner, Vlasov gradually began to cooperate with the Germans and eventually became the commander of the anti-communist Russian Liberation Army (ROA) in November 1944. However, after the war he was handed back to Soviet custody and executed as a traitor. (Nik Cornish at Stavka)

the end of the pocket in early July 1942, the Volkhov Front suffered 403,000 casualties – including almost 150,000 killed or captured. This was a frightening loss for negligible gains and it deprived the Soviets of the initiative on the Leningrad and Volkhov fronts for several months. The only significant gain that the Volkhov Front retained from the failed offensive was the large bulge pushed into the German lines at Pogost'e, which made the German-held Kirishi salient vulnerable to a pincer attack. Meretskov attacked this salient on 5–11 June and again on 20–26 July, but on each occasion the German 11. Infanterie-Division repulsed the equivalent of three enemy divisions. Yet the Kirishi salient was costing AOK 18 a great many casualties and Meretskov attacked it again in August. Although the German defences had held, it was clear to Küchler that Soviet offensives would only grow stronger unless something was done to change the balance of forces on the Leningrad front.

German options, summer 1942

With the defeat of the Soviet Lyuban Offensive, the Germans began to reconsider the wisdom of committing the bulk of Heeresgruppe Nord to an extended siege operation. Führer Directive 41, issued on 5 April 1942, reversed the previous decision to besiege Leningrad and directed Küchler to capture the city. The OKH assured Küchler that he would be provided sufficient reinforcements for a summer offensive. Once Sevastopol fell on 4 July, the bulk of Manstein's AOK 11 became available for redeployment and Hitler decided that four of its infantry divisions and its heavy artillery would be transferred to the Leningrad front.

In light of Führer Directive 41, Küchler's staff developed three main offensive plans regarding Leningrad for the summer of 1942: Operation *Nordlicht* (northern lights), Operation *Bettelstab* (beggar's staff) and Operation *Moorbrand* (moor fire). The last two were both relatively small-scale offensives, employing only three divisions; the first aimed at eliminating the Oranienbaum bridgehead and the other a pincer attack against the Pogost'e salient. However, *Nordlicht* was a major undertaking and would

Wrecks of Soviet BT-5 tanks litter the banks of the Volkhov River in summer 1942. Soviet armour was often forced to attack through very narrow mobility corridors in the swampy terrain and became easy prey for German *Panzerjäger* units. (Fonds of the RGKFD, Krasnogorsk)

not be feasible until Manstein's AOK 11 arrived. On 23 July, Führer Directive 45 specified that Leningrad should be captured by early September and recommended that the two smaller operations should be completed first to free up reserves for the main event.

Despite a window of opportunity in July–August, Heeresgruppe Nord remained on the defensive and decided to forego even a limited offensive until significant reinforcements arrived. Owing to transportation difficulties, Manstein's headquarters did not arrive on the Leningrad front until 27 August and his four infantry divisions (24., 132. and 170. Infanterie-Divisionen, and 28. Jäger-Division) began trickling in shortly afterwards. These AOK 11 divisions still retained the triangular nine-battalion structure and were much stronger than most of the reduced-size divisions in AOK 18. Küchler also received the 3. and 5. Gebirgsjäger-Divisionen from Norway and the Spanish 250. Infanterie-Division. Luftflotte I was reinforced to over 250 operational aircraft in July 1942. Once the forces began to assemble on the Leningrad front, Hitler decreed that Manstein's AOK 11 would conduct Operation *Nordlicht* with a total of nine divisions, while AOK 18 held the Volkhov. The offensive was tentatively expected to begin on 14 September and conclude by the end of the month.

A Soviet trench position preserved in the Oranienbaum bridgehead. Although the Soviets constructed multiple lines of fortifications within this enclave, the strength of its defences alone do not explain why the Germans allowed this anomaly to persist for over two years. Heeresgruppe Nord made numerous plans to crush the bridgehead in 1942/43 but failed to do so, with fatal consequences in 1944. (Phil Curme Collection)

After his costly victory at Sevastopol, Manstein was not sanguine about fighting his way into a major city like Leningrad defended by more than 200,000 Soviet troops. In particular, he lacked sufficient assault pioneers and assault guns – two of the critical force multipliers used at Sevastopol – to conduct effective urban combat operations. The original *Nordlicht* plan developed by AOK 18 staff called for a major breakthrough attack conducted by four divisions out of Pushkin – basically a continuation of the September 1941 attack – followed by a direct assault into the southern end of Leningrad. Instead, Manstein altered the plan by emphasizing envelopment rather than assault. In Manstein's revised *Nordlicht* plan, five German divisions would seize the Pulkovo Heights and then snip off the Kolpino salient, followed by an assault crossing of the Neva River. Once bridgeheads were established across the Neva, Manstein intended to push the 12. Panzer-Division and four infantry divisions across the river to roll up the Soviet 55th Army and then advance northwards towards the Leningrad–Osinevets railway line. If successful, Manstein's forces would cut all Soviet supply links across Lake Ladoga, thereby ensuring the rapid starvation of Leningrad's garrison. As usual, there was a great deal of risk in Manstein's plan since he had to strip Heeresgruppe Nord of virtually all reserves, leaving the Volkhov sector vulnerable to attack.

Amazingly, the Germans undertook no offensive actions against Leningrad at all during the summer of 1942. However, the besieged Soviet forces in Leningrad took no summer break. Fearing a renewed German push against Leningrad, Govorov ordered both the 42nd and 55th armies to conduct spoiling attacks against the German L AK lines. The 42nd Army

The Second Siniavino Offensive, 27 August–3 September 1942

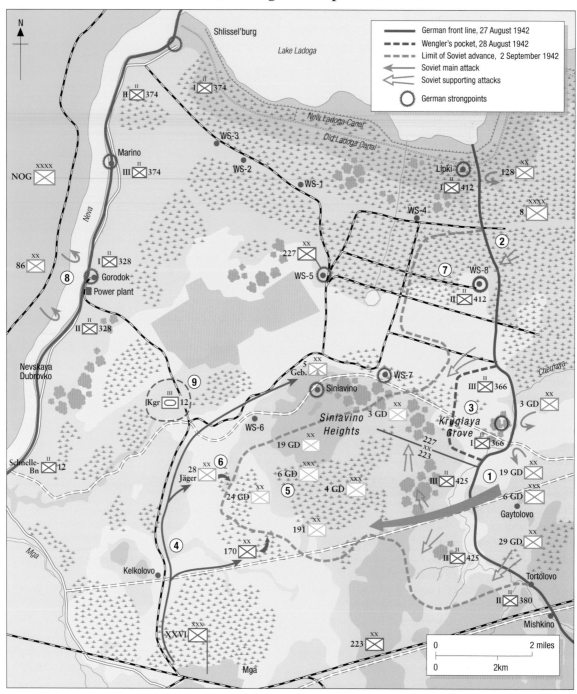

attacked the 215. Infanterie-Division near Uritsk on 20 July with two rifle divisions, followed by the 55th Army attacking the SS-Polizei-Division south of Kolpino on 23 July with a rifle division and a tank brigade. Both attacks gained a little ground against the complacent L AK and forced Küchler to divert some of the units forming up for *Nordlicht*, reinforcing the siege lines with 5. Gebirgsjäger-Division. However, AOK 18 quartermasters did use the summer months to build up supply bases at Siverskaya, Tosno and Lyuban,

1 27 August: at 0210hrs, the Soviet 8th Army begins its attack on the German XXVI AK in the Mga–Siniavino corridor. After an artillery preparation, the 6th Guards Rifle Corps crosses the Chernaya River and attacks near the junction of the 223. and 227. Infanterie-Divisionen boundaries. The 3rd Guards Rifle Division fails to capture the Kruglaya Grove from Oberst Wengler's Grenadier-Regiment 366, but the 19th Guards Rifle Division manages to overrun Grenadier-Regiment 425's forward defences and advances four kilometres. The 24th Guards Rifle Division captures Tortolovo.

2 27 August: the 128th Rifle Division launches supporting attacks on Lipki and Workers' Settlement No. 8 (WS-8).

3 28 August: Oberst Wengler's Grenadier-Regiment 366 is encircled in the Kruglaya Grove, but the 6th Guards Rifle Corps cannot eliminate this position.

4 28 August: Lindemann rushes up elements of the 28. Jäger-, 5. Gebirgsjäger- and 170. Infanterie-Divisionen to block the Soviet penetration.

5 30 August: the Soviet advance westwards has lost momentum, so Starikov commits the 4th Guards Rifle Corps to reinforce the main effort, but the German defence of the Siniavino Heights holds.

6 1/2 September: counterattacks by the 28. Jäger- and 170. Infanterie-Divisionen stop the 8th Army advance five kilometres from the Neva River.

7 2 September: the 128th Rifle Division succeeds in capturing WS-8, but any further advance is blocked.

8 3 September: the Neva Operational Group tries to assist Starikov's stalled advance by making another division-sized effort to cross the Neva River near Gorodok but it is easily repulsed.

9 27 August to 3 September: a regimental-sized Kampfgruppe from 12. Panzer-Division remains in reserve west of Siniavino, ready to counterattack any sudden Soviet breakthrough.

while engineers improved the road and rail network behind the lines. These logistical improvements would serve AOK 18 well during the defensive battles of 1942/43.

Second Siniavino Offensive, August 1942

Despite the dilatory offensive preparations by Heeresgruppe Nord, the Stavka was aware of Operation *Nordlicht* from intelligence sources and Stalin was determined to break the siege of Leningrad before the Germans could make their move. After the disastrous Lyuban Offensive, Meretskov was ordered to rebuild 2nd Shock Army, using remnants that had escaped the pocket and new reinforcements. He also began planning for a new offensive to break the siege, using a simpler, more direct approach and a great mass of artillery. With the Stavka's concurrence, Meretskov and Govorov agreed on a pincer attack, involving near-simultaneous assaults against the west and east sides of the narrowest portion of the German siege lines, around Siniavino. At this point, Meretskov's forces were only 17km from Govorov's forces on the Neva River and they calculated that they could attack and achieve a link-up before Küchler could reinforce the sector.

The east side of the Siniavino sector, already dubbed 'the corridor of death' since it was under Soviet artillery fire from both sides, was held by General der Artillerie Albert Wodrig's XXVI AK, with the 223. and 227. Infanterie-Divisionen. Wodrig had only seven infantry battalions defending a 15km front stretching from Lipki on Lake Ladoga to Mishkino,

LEFT
A group of about 30 German prisoners, captured during the Second Siniavino Offensive in late August 1942, are escorted to the rear by Soviet troops. Unlike other fronts, the Soviets never succeeded in bagging any large hauls of German prisoners in their repeated offensives around Leningrad. (Courtesy of the Central Museum of the Armed Forces, Moscow)

RIGHT
A Nebelwerfer 41 six-barrelled 150mm rocket launcher, probably from Nebelwerfer-Regiment 70, which came up from the Crimea with AOK 11 in August 1942. This unit was used to help repel the Soviet attack on the Siniavino Heights. (HITM Archives)

Bags of foodstuffs are transferred from a barge to a small-gauge train at Osinovets on 1 September 1942. During warm weather months, besieged Leningrad was completely dependent upon barge traffic across Lake Ladoga. (RIA Novosti)

with five other battalions holding the Neva Line. Owing to the reduction of the infantry divisions from nine to six battalions, Wodrig persuaded Küchler to 'loan' him five battalions from the 207. and 285. Sicherungs-Divisionen, but he still had a very weak force to hold the most critical terrain in the siege lines around Leningrad. The XXVI AK front was protected by a combination of fortified strongpoints, minefields, pre-planned artillery barrages and extensive swamps. Wodrig built his defences upon the stoutly built workers' settlements that had been built in this area before the war, with the key positions being Workers' Settlement 8 (WS-8), the Kruglaya Grove and the dominant Siniavino Heights. On the west side of the salient, the very experienced SS-Polizei-Division also held part of the Neva River front. Although Wodrig had no reserves, part of Manstein's AOK 11 was just arriving south of Leningrad for the upcoming Operation *Nordlicht*.

Once Soviet intelligence learned of the imminent arrival of Manstein's forces, the Stavka pressed Meretskov and Govorov to launch their offensives immediately, to forestall any possible German success at Leningrad. Govorov dutifully kicked off his part of the offensive by attempting to seize two crossings over the Neva on 19 August, but the SS-Polizei repulsed these efforts with heavy losses. Unlike the winter months, where the Soviets could send tanks and infantry across the frozen Neva, a cross-river attack in the summer was relatively easy for the Germans to defend against. However, Wodrig's corps was less well prepared for Meretskov's offensive, which began at 0210hrs on 27 August.

Meretskov's main effort was launched by General-Major Filipp N. Starikov's 8th Army in the Gaitolovo sector, near the boundary of the 223. and 227. Infanterie-Divisionen. Starikov's initial shock group consisted of three divisions of General-Major Sergei T. Biiakov's 6th Guards Rifle Corps, with the second echelon formed by General-Major Nikolai A. Gagen's 4th Guards Rifle Corps. Meretskov played by the book: he achieved a 4:1 advantage in infantry in a narrow five-kilometre-wide sector, and provided over 580 army-level howitzers,

120mm mortars and multiple rocket launchers to support the assault. Despite the superior mass and firepower, the 6th Guards Rifle Corps failed to capture the heavily defended Kruglaya Grove, but the 19th Guards Rifle Division was able to push its way three kilometres into the forwards defences of Grenadier-Regiment 425. As usual, by massing a rifle division against a single German battalion, the Soviets made a narrow breach, but the supporting attacks on the flanks were less successful. Starikov was limited to a narrow penetration battle – just as had happened to the 2nd Shock Army in the Lyuban Offensive. Furthermore, Küchler began to commit reserves more quickly than Meretskov had anticipated and Starikov's advance slowed to a crawl in successive days. Elements of the 5. Gebirgsjäger-Division and 28. Jäger-Division began to arrive on 28 August, followed by the 170. Infanterie-Division and four Tiger tanks of s.Pz.Abt. 502. Rather than cracking under the Soviet sledgehammer, German resistance was increasing. Even though two German battalions under Oberst Wengler were encircled in the Kruglaya Grove, Starikov's rifle units had great difficulty reducing this position.

Although the Soviets enjoyed a considerable superiority in artillery, the tactical execution of the offensive was seriously flawed. Rifle units were fed into battle piecemeal and the artillery was unable to identify and destroy the German main line of resistance, concealed in the heavily wooded terrain. Most Soviet artillery barrages were area fires, hindered by morning fog and inexperienced forward observers. Starikov ignored the terrain and sent his 124th Tank Brigade into swamps where 24 of its 27 tanks became mired and were then destroyed by German *Panzerjäger*. Furthermore, Meretskov failed to provide adequate engineer support to breach minefields and build corduroy roads over swamps, so Starikov's forces were limited to advancing along a single, narrow axis.

In frustration, Meretskov ordered Starikov to commit the 4th Guards Rifle Corps into the fight, and then gradually committed the 2nd Shock Army piecemeal to keep the advance going. Govorov finally managed to get some infantry across the Neva on 26 August, re-occupying the former 'five-kopeck bridgehead' lost in April, but could not advance any further. By 31 August, the 8th Army reached the south-east edge of the Siniavino Heights but was rapidly running out of steam. Counterattacks by the 28. Jäger-Division and 170. Infanterie-Division on 1/2 September stopped Starikov's spearheads five kilometres short of the link-up with the Nevskaya Dubrovka bridgehead. Once again, Meretskov stood to eliminate an entire German corps if he could only complete the encirclement, but Govorov's forces were unable to break out of their tiny bridgehead and Starikov no longer had the strength to advance. The Soviet offensive had stalled.

Manstein's counteroffensive, September 1942

At his forward headquarters at Vinnitsa in the Ukraine, Hitler was concerned that the Soviet Siniavino Offensive would succeed in disrupting the execution of *Nordlicht*, even though it was already apparent that it had failed to raise the siege of Leningrad. Hitler ordered Manstein to take over the battle around Siniavino and crush the Soviet penetration as rapidly as possible. In a rather awkward command arrangement, AOK 11 was put in charge of all German forces already around Siniavino, as well as the reinforcements just arriving from the Crimea, which temporarily reduced Lindemann's AOK 18 to a rump formation. In his haste to resolve the Soviet penetration quickly, Manstein's initial improvised effort to cut off the base of the salient was repulsed on 10

12 January 1943

1. 1200hrs: the Assault by 45th Guards Rifle Division across the Neva River is repulsed with heavy losses.
2. The attack by 86th Rifle Division across the Neva is also defeated.
3. The 136th and 268th rifle divisions succeed in overrunning Auflärüngs-Abteilung 240 at Marino and advance two to three kilometres eastwards. Soviet engineers begin building a pontoon bridge and by nightfall, the 61st Tank Brigade crosses the Neva to expand the bridgehead.
4. 1000–1200hrs: the 372nd Rifle Division makes three attacks, supported by armor, but fails to penetrate the defenses of GR 374 at WS-8.
5. 1300–1500hrs: the 128th Rifle Division attacks and succeeds in isolating the German battalion holding Lipki, which holds a near-impregnable position behind the canal.
6. 1700hrs: The 256th and 327th rifle divisions exploit weak spots in the German defences and succeed in capturing the north-east corner of the Kruglaya Woods.

13 January 1943

7. The 67th Army sends its 102nd and 123rd rifle brigades and 152nd Tank Brigade to capture Gorodok but they are repulsed by the 170. Infanterie-Division. German reinforcements arrive and launch a powerful counterattack that stops any further Soviet advances in this sector for the time being.
8. The 256th Rifle Division envelops WS-8, but the embattled German garrison holds out.
9. Infanterie-Regiment 284 from the 96. Infanterie-Division arrives in time to counterattack and slow down the Soviet breakout from Marino.

14 January 1943

10. 0700–0830hrs: the Soviet 55th Naval Infantry Brigade and 12th Ski Brigade begin conducting over-ice attacks against the northern flank of the 227. Infanterie-Division, but seize only a toehold.

11. The 2nd Shock Army begins attacks on WS-5 and WS-7 but fails to seize either one.
12. The 128th Rifle Division advances over one kilometre westwards but fails to seize WS-4 before German reinforcements arrive and create a new line.
13. The 45th Guards Rifle Division manages to cross the Neva and reoccupy the former five-kopeck bridgehead, but can advance no further.

15 January 1943

14. The 67th Army and 2nd Shock Army advance to within two kilometres of each other, nearly cutting off the Germans in Shlissel'burg. Two battalions of Gebirgsjäger-Regiment 100 arrive to stiffen the defences at WS-1 and WS-2.
15. The two battalions of Infanterie-Regiment 374 encircled in WS-8 breakout during the night and most of the troops manage to reach the German lines near WS-7.

16 January 1943

16. Kampfgruppe Hühner arrives to stiffen the German defence at WS-5 but is soon encircled as Soviet troops cut the road south of it.
17. The 86th Rifle Division, after crossing into the Marino bridgehead, begins attacking into Shlissel'burg.

17 January 1943

18. SS-Polizei-Regiment 1 arrives to stiffen the German defence on the Siniavino Heights and launches local counterattacks that keep the 136th Rifle Division off the high ground.
19. WS-3 is finally captured after days of relentless attacks by 67th Army.

18 January 1943

20. The 86th Rifle Division captures Shlissel'burg.
21. 0930hrs: the 136th Rifle Division and 61st Tank Brigade capture WS-5. Shortly thereafter, troops from the 67th Army and 2nd Shock Army link-up south of WS-1, opening a land corridor to Leningrad.

September. Manstein decided to wait until all his forces were in place and then launched a powerful pincer attack with four divisions from XXVI and XXX AK on 21 September, which succeeded in linking up near Gaitolovo within four days. The German counterattack succeeded in trapping the bulk of the Soviet 8th Army and part of the 2nd Shock Army in the pocket. Just after Starikov's forces were encircled, the 55th Army managed to get elements of two rifle divisions across the Neva River on 26 September, but it was too late. Manstein ordered the 12. Panzer-Division, which had 40 tanks, to counterattack and within days the Soviets had lost two of their three bridgeheads. Shortly thereafter, the 55th Army forces withdrew back across the Neva.

Manstein set about methodically reducing the pocket in late September, although mopping-up operations in the swamps continued until mid-October. At least 12,300 prisoners were taken and Meretskov's forces had taken another battering for no territorial gains. All told, the Leningrad and Volkhov fronts suffered 113,674 casualties in the offensive – about 59 per cent of their committed forces. Heeresgruppe Nord suffered 25,936 casualties during August–September 1942 and Manstein requested 10,500 replacements before his forces would be ready to execute *Nordlicht*. Some of the best units slated for *Nordlicht* were particularly hard hit, such as 5. Gebirgsjager-Division, which suffered 2,183 casualties and lost one-quarter of its horses. Although the OKH kept *Nordlicht* as an option for some time, it was effectively cancelled when Manstein and his AOK 11 staff were sent south to form Heeresgruppe Don in response to the Stalingrad crisis in November. While there is no doubt that the German defence of the Siniavino Heights was a major tactical success, the Soviets succeeded in pre-empting Operation *Nordlicht* and thereby saved Leningrad.

Operation *Spark*, 12–18 January 1943

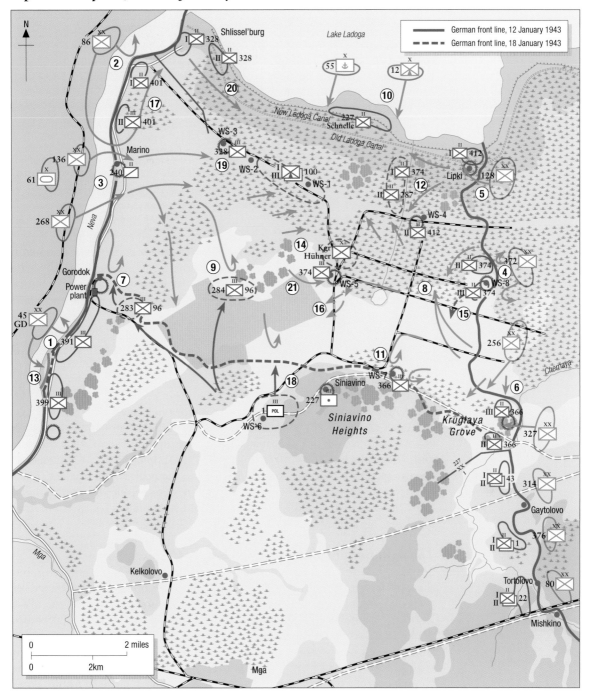

N

Lake Ladoga

| German front line, 12 January 1943 |
| German front line, 18 January 1943 |

Shlissel'burg
86
328
328
55
12
20
10
401
17
New Ladoga Canal
227
Schnelle
Old Ladoga Canal
401
WS-3
Marino
328
412
136
19
WS-2
100
Lipki
128
61
240
WS-1
374
3
287
12
5
268
WS-4
412
Neva
14
Ker
Hühner
372
Gorodok
9
374
374
4
Power
plant
7
284 96
21
WS-5
WS-8
374
283 96
16
8
45 GD
15
1
391
256
13
11
399
6
18
WS-7
366
366
227
Siniavino
327
Kruglaya
Grove
WS-6
Siniavino
Heights
366
314
43
Gaytolovo
376
1
Kelkolovo
Tortolovo
22
80
Mishkino
Mga
0   2 miles
0   2km
Mga
Chernaya

The second year of the siege

While counting on a successful relief effort, Govorov took advantage of Heeresgruppe Nord's inactivity during the summer of 1942 to prepare Leningrad for another winter siege. First and foremost, the Ladoga Flotilla was expanded and kept the supply lines to Leningrad open, despite Luftwaffe attacks. About 539,000 civilians and wounded were evacuated by boat across Lake Ladoga in the summer of 1942, leaving only 700,000 civilians and

420,000 military personnel in Leningrad. The evacuation not only saved lives but also helped to reduce the city's future food requirements and to build up reserves. Govorov also received thousands of replacements across the lake, enabling him to rebuild his badly depleted units. Once limited electricity was restored to the city, Leningrad's industries were able to resume some war production, focusing on tank/artillery repair and the manufacture of small arms, artillery ammunition and mines.

While Zhdanov reorganized and expanded the number of worker battalions to 52 to defend the inner city, Govorov set about completing the defence lines that had been thrown together in August 1941. More bunkers, trenches and obstacles were added throughout 1942, until both the 42nd Army and the 55th Army had three solid lines of defence. A special counterbattery unit was formed to challenge the German bombardment of Leningrad and it succeeded in driving some of the medium-calibre guns out of range of the inner city. If Manstein had mounted *Nordlicht* in September 1942, he would have found the Soviet defences far more formidable than they had been a year before.

Parts of the Leningrad Front were relatively quiet. The Oranienbaum salient was defended by the Coastal Operations Group (COG) with two rifle divisions and four brigades of riflemen and naval infantry. Küchler assigned two Luftwaffe field divisions from III Luftwaffe-Feld-Korps to guard Oranienbaum and he used this quiet backwater as a place to rotate battle-weary divisions from the Volkhov. North of Leningrad, the Soviet 23rd Army had three to four rifle divisions keeping an eye on the inactive Finns, which also provided Govorov with a quiet sector to rotate depleted units.

In the Gulf of Finland, the KBF was very active in 1942, conducting three major submarine breakout operations between June and October 1942. With assistance from the VVS, a number of submarines succeeded in getting past the mines and they sank 57,733 tons of Axis shipping. Alarmed by this Soviet submarine offensive, the Germans and Finns increased their mine barriers and ASW forces in the Gulf of Finland. In March 1943, the Kriegsmarine began Operation *Walroß*, laying a 48km long steel anti-submarine net across the narrowest part of the Gulf of Finland. Once the net and the Nashorn mine barrage were completed in May 1943, no further Soviet submarine breakouts succeeded until October 1944.

The fight for air superiority, 1942/43

Novikov was promoted to commander of the entire VVS in April 1942, but the units he had trained and organized in the winter of 1941/42 continued his policy of frequent raids on German front-line units, as well as the main Luftflotte I air bases at Krasnogvardeisk and Siverskaya. The Luftwaffe deployed a Freya radar to protect its forward air bases but it was unable to stop the recurrent strafing attacks on AOK 18, which caused much friction with Lindemann. By July 1942, Luftflotte I still held the edge in air-to-air combat over the battlefield, but it failed to shut off Soviet logistic traffic across Lake Ladoga and it was increasingly challenged by a resurgent VVS. The PVO had massed 59 flak batteries in an outer ring around the city and 71 flak batteries in an inner ring, which forced Luftflotte I to discontinue periodic large-scale bomber raids over Leningrad after April 1942. Meanwhile, based upon experience gained from the failed Lyuban offensive, the VVS-Volkhov Front units were reorganized into the 14th Air Army and the VVS-Leningrad Front into the 13th Air Army, but even including the VVS-KBF, these formations had only 450 operational aircraft by mid-1942.

A squad of German infantrymen checking their weapons before going on patrol in the winter of 1942/43. Although fairly well equipped for the weather, the German infantry in Heeresgruppe Nord were gradually being bled white by the recurrent Soviet offensives and receiving fewer and younger replacements as the siege dragged on. (Nik Cornish at Stavka)

In July 1942, I/JG 54 began receiving the upgraded Bf 109G fighter and inflicted great losses upon the 13th and 14th air armies in a series of battles along the Volkhov. On 2 August, Luftflotte I was even emboldened enough to conduct a rare 50-strong bomber raid over central Leningrad, in the hope of enticing the Soviet fighters into battle with JG 54. However, a powerful Soviet offensive against Heeresgruppe Mitte forced Luftflotte I to send many units southwards, allowing the VVS to operate more freely around Leningrad. When the second Siniavino Offensive began, JG 54 was too weak to prevent the 14th Air Army from sending close support groups of Il-2 Sturmoviks over the battlefield in the opening days of the attack. Alarmed by the strength of the Soviet offensive, the OKL rushed reinforcements from Germany to Luftflotte I, including I/JG 51 with the new Fw 190 fighter. On 1 September, Luftflotte I appeared in strength over the Siniavino battlefield and its fighters began to methodically shoot the 14th Air Army to pieces. After just a few days of intense air combat, Soviet aircraft virtually disappeared over the front and German bombers were able to support Manstein's counterattack without interference. During September 1942, Luftflotte I claimed 292 VVS aircraft for the loss of only six fighters and 28 other aircraft. Eight bomber *Gruppen* were concentrated to bomb the trapped 2nd Shock Army into submission. Yet as soon as the Soviet offensive was defeated, Luftflotte I had to return most of its reinforcements and it was again reduced to a handful of squadrons. As Luftwaffe power in the region ebbed, AOK 18 became increasingly vulnerable to Soviet air attacks, which made a successful relief of Leningrad more likely.

All told, Luftflotte I lost 267 aircraft in 1942 and claimed 2,146 Soviet aircraft destroyed, representing an 8:1 air-to-air kill ratio. However, the VVS was able to conduct over 56,000 sorties on the Leningrad–Volkhov axis in 1942 – almost three times as many as the Luftwaffe.

That the Soviets did not gain complete air superiority over the entire region was due in part to the technical superiority of the Fw 190A fighter and the dominance of a few Jagdflieger, such as Leutnant Walter Nowotny. Already a successful ace with 62 victories by February 1943, once equipped with the new Fw 190 fighter Nowotny went on a killing spree in mid-1943

THE CAPTURE OF TIGER 100, 18 JANUARY 1943 (pp. 66–67)

On the morning of 18 January 1943, the spearheads of the Soviet 67th Army (Leningrad Front) and 2nd Shock Army (Volkhov Front) linked up near Workers' Settlement No. 1, re-opening a land corridor to Leningrad. This Soviet success also trapped about 8,000 German troops from Kampfgruppe Hühner, including a group of Tiger tanks from 1./s.Pz.Abt. 502. The German troops immediately began fighting their way south trying to escape the encirclement and most succeed in reaching German lines, but four Tigers were lost to enemy action. Just south of Workers' Settlement No. 5, Tiger 100 accidentally drove off the trail and became mired in a peat bog. The German tankers hurriedly tried to prepare the tank for demolition but before they could accomplish this, pursuing Soviet infantry arrived in force and drove them off. Soviet troops **(1)** quickly mounted onto Tiger 100 **(2)** and began to throw out the

demolition charges. The Germans mounted a counterattack to try and reach the immobilized Tiger but were driven back with heavy losses, including several PzKpfw III medium tanks knocked out by Soviet anti-tank guns. Seizing the moment, local Soviet commanders quickly ordered five light T-60 tanks **(3)** from the 61st Tank Brigade to the site. The Soviet tankers managed to attach tow cables **(4)** from all five T-60s to the Tiger and, since it had been left in neutral, they were able to get it rolling. Finally, the Soviets succeeded in dragging Tiger 100 far enough out of the bog that it was practical for a KV-1 tank to tow it back to their own lines. This was the first intact Tiger captured on the Eastern Front and the Soviet technical evaluation helped to spur the development of the IS series of heavy tanks.

that resulted in the destruction of 135 Soviet aircraft in a four-month period. It is rare that a single individual warrior can have an operational-level impact, but Nowotny's skill helped to frustrate the Soviet 13th Air Army's ability to deliver effective air support during the bloody battles around Siniavino in August 1943. However, even Nowotny could not stave off the inevitable and by October 1943, IV/JG 54 was the only German fighter unit operating around Leningrad, with just 22 Bf 109Gs and four Fw 190s. At the same time, the 13th and 14th air armies had grown to a total of over 800 aircraft, including 400 fighters. Against these odds, Luftflotte I was no longer able to contest seriously the airspace over the battlefield and the Luftwaffe sorties dropped off to negligible levels by November 1943, which played a great role in the Soviet ability to finally break the siege.

THE SIEGE WEAKENS, 1943

Both sides shifted to the defensive after the failure of the Second Siniavino Offensive and remained that way for three months. The Stavka's attention was focused on the developing drama around Stalingrad and the Volkhov Front was too weak to mount another offensive until the 2nd Shock Army could be rebuilt (again). However, Govorov and Meretskov began working on plans for a new joint offensive in December, which envisioned another pincer attack on the Siniavino corridor. Since one of the main faults of the previous effort was the inability of the NOG to gain significant bridgeheads across the Neva, Govorov reorganized the NOG as the 67th Army and strengthened it with fresh rifle and artillery units. Meanwhile, Meretskov received five rifle divisions, an engineer brigade and three ski brigades, plus considerable artillery, which he used to rebuild 2nd Shock Army. Meretskov and Govorov decided to attack in early January 1943, once the Neva River was frozen solid enough to allow tanks to cross. This time, both fronts would attack simultaneously, preventing the Germans from shifting reserves to defeat each in turn. Although logistical preparations were still hindered by transportation shortages, Meretskov was given far more time to prepare this offensive than his previous efforts and his forces were much better prepared. However, two days before the offensive began, General Zhukov arrived at Meretskov's headquarters as the Stavka representative.

Lindemann's AOK 18 still held the Siniavino salient with its XXVI AK, but the amount of reserves available to confront another Soviet offensive had

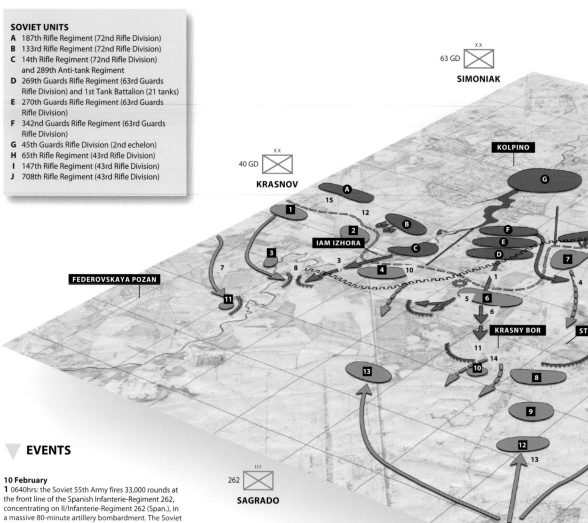

SOVIET UNITS
A 187th Rifle Regiment (72nd Rifle Division)
B 133rd Rifle Regiment (72nd Rifle Division)
C 14th Rifle Regiment (72nd Rifle Division)
and 289th Anti-tank Regiment
D 269th Guards Rifle Regiment (63rd Guards
Rifle Division) and 1st Tank Battalion (21 tanks)
E 270th Guards Rifle Regiment (63rd Guards
Rifle Division)
F 342nd Guards Rifle Regiment (63rd Guards
Rifle Division)
G 45th Guards Rifle Division (2nd echelon)
H 65th Rifle Regiment (43rd Rifle Division)
I 147th Rifle Regiment (43rd Rifle Division)
J 708th Rifle Regiment (43rd Rifle Division)

63 GD
SIMONIAK

40 GD
KRASNOV

KOLPINO

IAM IZHORA

FEDEROVSKAYA POZAN

KRASNY BOR

STEPA

▼ EVENTS

10 February
1 0640hrs: the Soviet 55th Army fires 33,000 rounds at the front line of the Spanish Infanterie-Regiment 262, concentrating on II/Infanterie-Regiment 262 (Span.), in a massive 80-minute artillery bombardment. The Soviet 13th Air Army conducts Il-2 Sturmovik attacks on Spanish forward positions.

2 0800hrs: I/Infanterie-Regiment 262 (Span.) repulses the initial attack by the 43rd Rifle Division.

3 0845hrs: two regiments of the 72nd Rifle Division overruns part of Feldersatz Bataillon 250 and advances along east bank of Izhora River. Local Spanish counterattacks are crushed.

4 0900hrs: the second attack on I/Infanterie-Regiment 262 (Span.) succeeds in penetrating both flanks and the battalion is nearly encircled. The survivors retreat southwards.

5 0930hrs: in the 55th Army's main effort, the 63rd Guards Rifle Division and the 31st Guards Tank Regiment penetrate the Spanish centre, blasting through the II/Infanterie-Regiment 262 (Span.) positions and head south towards Krasny Bor. Other Soviet troops envelope El Bastion and push II/Infanterie-Regiment 262 (Span.) remnants back towards the highway.

6 1100hrs: the Spanish form a temporary line on the outskirts of Krasny Bor and succeed in knocking out four Soviet tanks. However, Soviet tanks and infantry soon fight their way into the northern part of the town.

262
SAGRADO

7 The 250. Infanterie-Division (Span.) commander shifts I/Infanterie-Regiment 263 (Span.) and part of the Infanterie-Regiment 269 east to establish new blocking positions along the Izhora.

8 1130hrs: the 14th and 133rd rifle regiments reach Staraya Myza but have suffered over 60 per cent casualties and can advance no further.

9 1130hrs: the SS-Polizei sends a mixed *Kampfgruppe* to protect its west flank due to the Spanish collapse.

10 Some Spanish positions in the centre manage to hold out all day but withdraw south at nightfall.

11 1300hrs: heavy fighting in Krasny Bor between the 63rd Guards Rifle Division and Spanish artillerymen and engineers.

12 1300hrs: III/Infanterie-Regiment 262 (Span.) defends the area around the Paper Mill and repulses several attacks from the 72nd Rifle Division, supported by armour.

13 1500hrs: Kampfgruppe Heckel arrives south of Krasny Bor and digs in. Grenadier-Regiment 316 marches west to the Red Woods while Grenadier-Regiment 374 marches east to Mishkino.

390
HECKEL

14 1700hrs: The last Spanish troops pull out of Krasny Bor. By nightfall, the Soviets have occupied Mishkino and Stepanovka.

11 February
15 0800hrs: III/Infanterie-Regiment 262 (Span.) repulses a final attack by the 72nd Rifle Division against the Paper Mill, inflicting heavy losses.

16 s.Pz.Abt. 502 (three Tigers and three PzKpfw III tanks) defeats a Soviet attack east from Mishkino toward Nikol'skoye, knocking out 32 tanks.

THE BATTLE OF KRASNY BOR, 10 FEBRUARY 1943

The Leningrad Front mounts a full-scale attack upon the Spanish Blue Division at Krasny Bor, with the intent of breaking through to Tosno and linking up with attacking Soviet forces from the Volkhov Front.

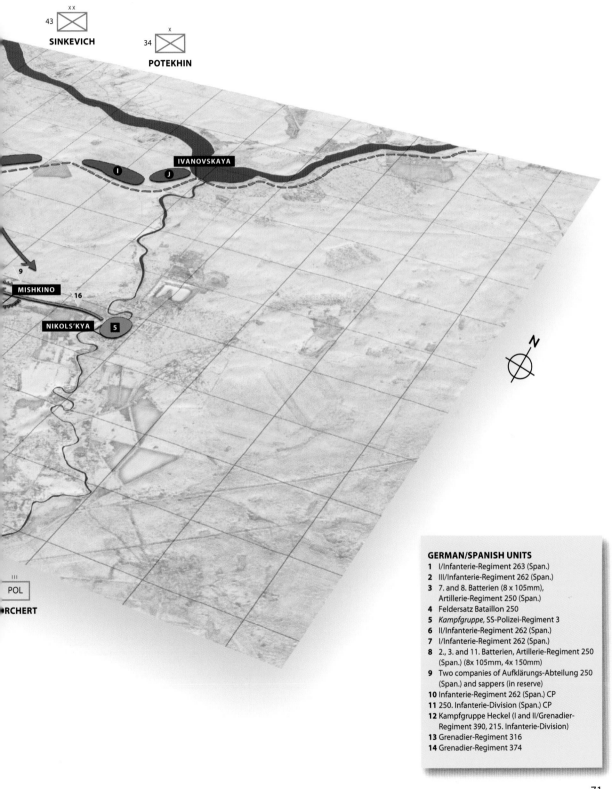

GERMAN/SPANISH UNITS
1 I/Infanterie-Regiment 263 (Span.)
2 III/Infanterie-Regiment 262 (Span.)
3 7. and 8. Batterien (8 x 105mm),
   Artillerie-Regiment 250 (Span.)
4 Feldersatz Bataillon 250
5 *Kampfgruppe*, SS-Polizei-Regiment 3
6 II/Infanterie-Regiment 262 (Span.)
7 I/Infanterie-Regiment 262 (Span.)
8 2., 3. and 11. Batterien, Artillerie-Regiment 250
   (Span.) (8x 105mm, 4x 150mm)
9 Two companies of Aufklärungs-Abteilung 250
   (Span.) and sappers (in reserve)
10 Infanterie-Regiment 262 (Span.) CP
11 250. Infanterie-Division (Span.) CP
12 Kampfgruppe Heckel (I and II/Grenadier-
   Regiment 390, 215. Infanterie-Division)
13 Grenadier-Regiment 316
14 Grenadier-Regiment 374

Боевой привет
шлет родина
ГЕРОИЧЕСКОМУ
ЛЕНИНГРАДУ!

Братский привет городу Ленина от №-ной
Армии, связавшего Ленинград с...

After the success of Operation *Istra* in opening up a land corridor to Leningrad, the first train arrived in the Finland Station on the morning of 7 February 1943. The engine is adorned with pictures of Molotov and Stalin, as well as slogans extolling the bravery of the population of Leningrad in the struggle with the German fascists. (Fonds of the RGKFD, Krasnogorsk)

dwindled as units (including 12. Panzer-Division) were transferred to other endangered fronts. The XXVI AK, now under General Ernst von Leyser, had the 170. Infanterie-Division and Grenadier-Regiment 328 from the 227. Infanterie-Division facing west to defend the Neva River front, while the remainder of the 227. Infanterie-Division, the 1. and 223. Infanterie-Divisionen faced east to defend the approaches to Mga and Siniavino.

At 0930hrs on 12 January 1943, both the Leningrad and Volkhov fronts commenced a 140-minute artillery preparation against the front-line positions of the German XXVI AK. Govorov committed 1,873 guns and mortars in the 67th Army sector and Meretskov committed 2,885 guns and mortars in the sectors of the 2nd Shock Army and 8th Army. Although the barrages hit to a depth of only three kilometres into the German front line, the defenders were badly shaken by a barrage that greatly exceeded previous efforts. Furthermore, the Soviet 13th and 14th air armies committed over 800 aircraft to the offensive, including swarms of Il-2 Sturmoviks that went after the German artillery.

After a final volley of rockets, the Soviet assault groups – formed into mixed rifle, tank and engineer teams – moved forwards in the chilling -9 degree Fahrenheit air towards the German forward positions. On the Neva, General-Lieutenant Mikhail Dukhanov's 67th Army attacked across the 600m-wide frozen river with four rifle divisions on a 12km-wide front between Shlissel'burg and Dubrovka. In the south, the 45th Guards Rifle Division's lead assault waves were virtually shot to pieces by MG42 machine-gun and mortar fire from Grenadier-Regiment 399, which held the area around Dubrovka and the Gorodok hospital. After several attempts, the Soviet infantry succeeded in reaching the German first trench line, but could go no further. Likewise, in the north, the 86th Rifle Division's attack on Shlissel'burg collapsed under the fire of a single German battalion, I/Grenadier-Regiment 401. However, Dukhanov's forces finally found a weak spot in the centre around Marino, held by Aufklärungs-Abteilung 240. Here 300 Germans repulsed several attacks by ten battalions of the 136th and 268th rifle divisions, inflicting about 3,000 casualties, but eventually the Soviet riflemen succeeded in getting enough men and a few T-60 light tanks across the river to overrun the forward German positions. By nightfall,

Spanish troops moving into positions near Krasny Bor in late January 1943. The transfer of part of the SS-Polizei-Division to hold the vital Siniavino Heights required the Spanish 250. Infanterie-Division to extend its front towards Krasny Bor, which made it an obvious target for a Soviet offensive in February. (Nik Cornish at Stavka)

Marino had been captured and these two divisions had secured a bridgehead five kilometres wide and three kilometres deep. Soviet engineers built several bridges across the Neva by nightfall, enabling 25 T-34 tanks from the 61st Tank Brigade to cross into the bridgehead. The 170. Infanterie-Division formed a hedgehog around the hospital and power station at Gorodok, barring the way to any further Soviet advance southwards.

Meanwhile, General-Lieutenant Vladimir Romanovsky's 2nd Shock Army attacked with six rifle divisions across a ten-kilometre-wide front, but failed to achieve more than limited penetration into the forward German defensive zone. The 128th Rifle Division succeeded in driving I/Grenadier-Regiment 374 out of WS-4, but II/Grenadier-Regiment 374 repulsed five attacks by the 372nd Rifle Division on WS-8. This stronghold consisted of 56 buildings, surrounded by a double line of trenches, barbed wire and minefields. In the centre, the 327th Rifle Division, supported by KV tanks, succeeded in capturing Kruglaya Grove, while the 256th Rifle Division advanced into the narrow gap between the grove and WS-8 and boldly advanced several kilometres westwards. However, Oberst Maximilian Wengler's Grenadier-Regiment 366 held a strong fortified position at WS-7 that squarely blocked the Soviet advance towards Siniavino. Furthermore, while the Soviets hovered around the edges of WS-8, the Germans were able to mount a local counterattack that recaptured part of the Kruglaya Grove. Even worse, the German strongpoints maintained radio contact with their supporting artillery, which now began to plaster the massed Soviet assault forces.

Leyser reacted to the Soviet offensive by dispatching most of his reserves – five infantry battalions from 96. Infanterie-Division, an 88mm flak battery and four Tiger tanks of 1./s.Pz.Abt. 502 – to buck up the faltering 170. Infanterie-Division at Gorodok. Since the main front appeared to be holding, Leyser ordered the 227. and 1. Infanterie-Divisionen to launch local counterattacks to limit any further Soviet advances while he focused most of his effort on crushing the 67th Army's fragile bridgehead before it was reinforced. Lindemann dispatched Kampfgruppe Hühner (Grenadier-Regimenter 151 and 162 from 61. Infanterie-Division), as well as elements of the SS-Polizei-Division and the 5. Gebirgsjäger Division to reinforce Leyser's hard-pressed corps.

On the second day of the offensive, the 67th Army made some progress, as General-Major Nikolai Simoniak's 136th Rifle Division and the 61st Light Tank Brigade advanced four kilometres eastwards. By nightfall, Dukhanov's spearhead was within five kilometres of 2nd Shock Army's forward units. However, the Soviet attack on the Gorodok power station failed and the 170. Infanterie-Division launched a powerful counterattack at 1630hrs that threw the 268th Rifle Division back two kilometres. One Tiger was set on fire after repeated hits, but 1./s.Pz.Abt. 502 destroyed 12 T-34 tanks, discouraging further Soviet attacks in this sector. On Romanovsky's front, progress was slow and Zhukov was constantly pressurizing Meretskov to advance more quickly, so he ordered 2nd Shock Army to commit its second-echelon divisions prematurely. Romanovsky's reinforced assault groups were able to encircle the battalion strongpoint at WS-8, but they could not crack the defence. Incredibly, a single encircled German infantry battalion at WS-8 held off the bulk of two rifle divisions, thanks to plentiful artillery support. Furthermore, an onset of poor weather greatly reduced Soviet air and artillery support, giving the Germans a brief respite to bring in more reinforcements.

The next four days, from 14 to 17 January, were marked by very heavy fighting as the 67th Army gradually expanded its bridgehead across the Neva and began to envelop Shlissel'burg from the south. Dukhanov committed all his second-echelon units and succeeded in making progress towards the north-east, but his troops were firmly blocked by the strong German defence at Gorodok. In the east, the surrounded II/GR 374 at WS-8 finally ran out of ammunition after four days of fighting, but in a daring move most of the troops escaped through the 2nd Shock Army's porous lines on the night of 15 January and reached German lines near Siniavino. Owing in large part to the dogged defence of WS-7 and WS-8, Romanovsky's advance was reduced to a crawl, but the gap between the two Soviet armies narrowed to only a few kilometres. The Germans now held a tenuous corridor along the only decent trail that ran north–south through the peat bogs from Siniavino to Shlissel'burg, centred on WS-5. Leyser ordered Kampfgruppe Hühner to hold WS-5 at all costs.

Soviet fortunes changed on the morning of 18 January, when the 67th Army finally achieved a link-up with the 2nd Shock Army near WS-1 at 0930hrs. Shortly thereafter, Simoniak's 136th Rifle Division and the 61st Tank Brigade fought their way into WS-5 and by 1400hrs the 86th Rifle Division captured Shlissel'burg. Although the Soviets trapped over 8,000 German troops inside the Shlissel'burg pocket, including Kampfgruppe

Hühner, they were unable to prevent their escape. In an amazing display of tactical skill, Hühner organized all the German units in the pocket and began an immediate breakout to the south. In two days of desperate fighting, most of Hühner's command succeeded in reaching the Siniavino Heights, although they lost their heavy equipment, including five Tiger tanks. Meanwhile, thanks to the time gained by the defence of WS-8, Lindemann was able to cobble together a new defensive line on the Siniavino Heights, formed from pioneers from the 96. Infanterie-Division, a dozen PzKpfw III tanks, as well as elements of SS-Polizei-Division and 28. Jäger-Division. Dukhanov's 67th Army began pounding on the western end of the line at the Gorodok hospital on 20 January, just as Romanovsky's units began attacking the east end of the line at WS-7, but the German defences held firm. Over the next few days, parts of three more German divisions arrived, strengthening the defence, while Soviet strength ebbed. Despite Zhukov's threats, the Soviet offensive finally petered out by the end of January.

Operation *Spark* had produced the first real Soviet success – albeit limited – in weakening the German blockade of Leningrad. Soviet losses had been very heavy; the 67th and 2nd Shock armies suffered 115,082 casualties, including 33,940 dead and missing, over a 19-day period. During 12–19 January, the German XXVI AK suffered 8,905 casualties, including 1,630 killed and 1,546 missing. Meretskov and Govorov succeeded in re-opening a narrow eight to ten-kilometre-wide land corridor to Leningrad and Soviet engineers laid a new railway line across the swampy terrain in two weeks. On 6 February 1943, the first Soviet train used the line to reach Leningrad. German artillery kept the railway line under bombardment and inflicted significant losses, rendering the corridor difficult to use, but it was a clear sign that the blockade was weakening.

Krasny Bor and the Fourth Siniavino Offensive, February 1943

Despite the partial success of Operation *Spark*, Stalin and Zhukov were exuberant in late January 1943 owing to the impending surrender of the German AOK 6 at Stalingrad and Soviet successes in getting across the Don River. This appeared to be the moment to launch a general winter counteroffensive, while German forces were stretched to the breaking point. Accordingly, Zhukov planned for a grand envelopment operation known as *Polar Star* against Heeresgruppe Nord, that would use the Leningrad and Volkhov fronts to pin Lindemann's AOK 18, while Marshal Timoshenko's North-west Front attacked with six armies to eliminate the Demyansk salient and then drove north-westwards to Luga. Zhukov envisioned that this multi-front offensive would trap the bulk of AOK 16 and 18 in a giant pocket south of Leningrad.

In order to increase the odds for his plan to succeed, Zhukov directed the Leningrad and Volkhov fronts to begin their own offensives first, in order to draw German reserves northwards, while in fact, the main Soviet effort was actually coming against AOK 16 south of Lake Il'men. Both Meretskov and Govorov realized that their forces were still depleted from heavy losses during Operation *Spark*, but they planned a series of set-piece attacks that would contribute to Zhukov's intent. With luck, Meretskov believed that another pincer attack by both armies might succeed in eliminating the Siniavino salient. As the left pincer, the 55th Army would attack out of Kolpino, crushing the Spanish 250. Infanterie-Division that had just occupied positions at Krasny Bor, and then advancing south-east to Tosno. The right pincer comprised the 54th Army, which would attack the German XXVIII AK and link up with the 55th Army near Tosno. Both the 67th Army and the 2nd Shock Army would conduct supporting attacks around Siniavino to tie down as many German units as possible.

The offensive began with a division-sized attack by the 55th Army that pushed back some of the Spanish outposts on 8 February, alerting Lindemann that another Soviet offensive was imminent. The main event began two days later. After heavy artillery preparations, the 54th and 55th armies attacked simultaneously on the morning of 10 February. The 55th Army attacked across a 14km front, but the main effort concentrated three reinforced rifle divisions and a tank brigade against a single regiment of the Spanish 250. Infanterie-Division, which was particularly weak in anti-tank defences. Massed Soviet artillery fire pulverized many of the forward Spanish positions, creating gaps into which tank–infantry assault groups quickly rushed. In a few hours, the 63rd Guards Rifle Division had fought its way into Krasny Bor

and Mishkino, where Spanish rear-area troops and engineers desperately fought to fend off encroaching T-34 tanks. On the Soviet left, the 43rd Rifle Division attacked one regiment of the SS-Polizei-Division, but failed to make a breakthrough. Strangely, the Soviets were somewhat lethargic after their initial success against the Spanish centre, which allowed the Germans to rush in three Kampfgruppen to create a new line south of Krasny Bor. By the time the Soviets were ready to resume their advance the next day, three Tiger tanks from 1./s.Pz.Abt. 502 were brought up to support the SS-Polizei and they quickly knocked out over 30 Soviet tanks. After three days the 55th Army was fought out, having advanced five kilometres at a cost of over 10,000 casualties. While the Spanish troops fought tenaciously, they suffered 3,645 casualties, which effectively destroyed one of the division's three regiments and wrecked their morale. Afterwards, Lindemann told Küchler that 'I don't trust the Spaniards any longer', and requested that they be replaced.

In conjunction with the 55th Army's attack, the 54th Army attacked the German 96. Infanterie-Division with four rifle divisions, three rifle brigades and a tank brigade on 10 February. Despite the heavy odds in their favour, the Soviet attack quickly bogged down and advanced only three kilometres in three days. In one action, the 4. SS-Legion 'Nederland' fought the Soviet 124th Tank Brigade to a standstill. A Dutch *Panzerjäger* company equipped with 75mm Pak 97/38 guns firing hollow-charge shells succeeded in knocking out 19 Soviet tanks, for which SS-Sturmmann Gerardus Mooyman became the first non-German to receive the Knight's Cross. Once again, Lindemann was able to shift just enough battalions from quiet sectors to keep his front from cracking. To make the German situation more difficult, the 67th Army and 2nd Shock Army joined the offensive on 12 February, launching set-piece attacks against Gorodok and Siniavino. While the 2nd Shock Army failed to make any progress against Siniavino, the 67th Army succeeded in capturing Gorodok after six days of heavy fighting. Overall, the offensive had dented the German lines, but only at the cost of significant losses. Furthermore, the Germans anticipated Zhukov's grand stroke by evacuating the Demyansk Salient on 19 February, thereby shortening the 16's front considerably. Timoshenko's last-minute attempt to modify the offensive to match the German re-positioning only resulted in a costly, botched effort. Zhukov's did not get his breakthrough south of Lake Il'men, nor could he encircle Heeresgruppe Nord.

Unsatisfied with his failure to exploit the success of Operation *Spark* and expand the land bridge to Leningrad, Zhukov ordered Govorov and Meretskov to try again in March. On 19 March, the 55th and 8th armies

LEFT
A Luftwaffe-manned 88mm Flak 18 in a firing position, probably well behind the German main line of resistance. Soviet attackers often were unaware of these positions until they achieved a breakthrough, and then ran into prepared anti-tank defences. (HITM Archives)

RIGHT
A Waffen-SS MG42 machine-gun team waiting in a reserve trench in the Leningrad area, summer 1943. Note the container for the spare barrel on the gunner's back. (HITM Archives)

LIBERATION OF THE PETERHOF, 20 JANUARY 1944 (pp. 78–79)

The Germans occupied the tsar's old summer palace of the Peterhof on 23 September 1941 and, during the siege, a number of German heavy artillery batteries used to shell Leningrad were hidden in the wooded parks near the palace. Virtually all of the art treasures, furniture and other valuables from the palace were looted and taken to Germany in 1942. Troops from the German 58th Infantry Division cut down most of the trees in the upper garden surrounding the palace, which was itself converted into a barracks until Soviet counterbattery fire set part of it alight. Eventually, the Germans converted the palace grounds into a fortress, laying mines on the walkways, digging trenches across the gardens, constructing wooden bunkers from the trees and fencing the area off with barbed wire. However, the German occupation of the Peterhof came to an abrupt end in January 1944 when the 2nd Shock Army began its successful breakout from the Oranienbaum bridgehead. The 9. Luftwaffe-Feld-Division, which occupied the coastal sector around the Peterhof, was quickly overwhelmed by the Soviet juggernaut and fell apart in a matter of days. This scene depicts the liberation of the ruined Peterhof palace (1) on 20 January 1943 by a tank-infantry group of the 2nd Shock Army. Rear echelon units of the 9. Luftwaffe-Feld-Division were still holding this area, but resistance was crumbling and most Germans were retreating southwards before they were completely encircled by the Soviet pincers. A T-34/76 tank (2) is advancing through the upper garden . Squads of Soviet infantry are fanning out behind the tank, taking the occupants of a German medical aid station prisoner (3). Meanwhile, other Germans flee from the advancing Soviet troops. The courtyard of the palace itself is littered with the wreckage of the German retreat (4).

attacked simultaneously, hoping to push their way through German lines to link up south of Mga. However, the German defences were still far too formidable and Lindemann was able to cull together reserves from quiet sectors. After achieving a small, three-kilometre-deep penetration south of Krasny Bor, the 55th Army's spearheads were thrown back by a fierce counterattack from the Legion Flandern and four Tigers from 1./s.Pz.Abt 502. In three days of combat, the four Tigers knocked out 40 Soviet tanks. Likewise, the Soviet 8th Army made a minor bulge in the German front line but then the arrival of even modest German reinforcements brought the entire advance to a halt. Zhukov – who had already left on 17 March – continued to berate Govorov and Meretskov to throw more forces into the offensive in order to achieve a breakthrough. Yet no breakthrough was achieved and after incurring another 150,000 casualties, the Stavka finally ordered the Leningrad and Volkhov fronts to shift to the defensive on 2 April.

In retaliation for the Soviet offensives, Harko 303 resumed its bombardment of Leningrad in full vigour in April, concentrating on military-industrial targets. Eisenbahn-Artillerie-Batterie 688 (two K5 28cm guns) fired 80 rounds at a concealed ammunition dump near Piskarevka, while Batterie 695 (one 'Kurz Bruno' 28cm gun) fired 60 rounds into the Bolshevik tank factory. German

A German le.FH18 105mm howitzer battery in position near Leningrad in the summer of 1943. By this point, AOK 18 had to reduce its battery size from four guns to three guns each since it couldn't replace losses and consequently, had only 531 105mm howitzers equipping its 168 division-level light artillery batteries. Thus German division-level artillery got weaker as the siege dragged on. (HITM Archives)

artillery also targeted the 42nd Army's command post (126 rounds from 15cm to 21cm), the Baltic shipyard (400 rounds 155mm), the Marti and Sudomek shipyards (each 250 rounds of 155mm), the Kirov tank plant (400 rounds of 15cm to 17cm) and the Farmakon explosives factory (500 rounds of 15cm to 17cm).

The struggle for the Siniavino Heights, July–September 1943
After the failure of the Fourth Siniavino Offensive, the Stavka's attention shifted towards the developing situation around Kursk and allowed the Leningrad and Volkhov fronts to shift to the defensive for a period of nearly four months. Govorov and Meretskov used this respite to rebuild and refit their badly depleted rifle units and to prepare for the next round. During the spring of 1943, the OKH kept *Nordlicht* and *Moorbrand* as possible offensive options for Heeresgruppe Nord to reverse the Soviet gains from Operation *Spark*. Küchler and Lindemann developed a revised plan, known as *Parkplatz*, that envisioned an offensive north from Siniavino to recapture Shlissel'burg and Lipki, thereby closing the land corridor to Leningrad.

14 January
1. 1040hrs: After a massive artillery preparation, the 2nd Shock Army attacks III SS-Panzer-Korps defences around Oranienbaum. The 122nd Rifle Corps overruns the 18. Regiment of 9. Luftwaffe-Feld-Division while the 43rd Rifle Corps pushes in the right flank of the 10. Luftwaffe-Feld-Division.
2. The 11. SS-Panzergrenadier-Division 'Nordland' commits several battalion-sized units into the flank of the 43rd Rifle Corps, but fails to seal off the Soviet penetration.

15 January
3. The 42nd Army begins a massive attack on the defences of L AK between Uritsk and the Pulkovo Heights. Simoniak's 30th Guards Rifle Corps achieves a four-kilometre-deep penetration into the 170. Infanterie-Division's defences in the centre.
4. The battleship *October Revolution* and other units of the Baltic Fleet pound the German positions around Uritsk with heavy naval gunfire.
5. The German AOK 18 commits its sole reserve unit, the 61. Infanterie-Division, to hold Ropsha.
6. The 2nd Shock Army sends the Oskotsky Mobile Group, based around the 152nd Tank Brigade, towards Ropsha but a German counterattack stalls the advance.

17 January
7. The 152nd Tank Brigade captures Glyadino and begins to envelop Ropsha from the west.
8. The 90th Rifle Division captures Dyatlitsy.
9. A German counterattack repulses the 42nd Army's mobile group, formed from the 1st and 220th tank brigades.
10. The 43rd Rifle Division advances towards Ropsha, while the 168th and 196th rifle divisions begin to push north towards the Peterhof.

18 January
11. The 189th Rifle Division advances towards Ropsha while the 30th Guards Rifle Corps drives into Krasnoye Selo. L AK begins withdrawing towards Krasnogvardeisk.

19 January
12. The 43rd Rifle Division and 189th Rifle Division fight their way into Ropsha and achieve a link-up of the two armies, isolating German forces around the Peterhof.
13. The German 126. Infanterie-Division and coastal units abandon the heavy artillery around the Peterhof and exfiltrate through Soviet lines during the night of 19/20 January.

The Soviet breakout from Oranienbaum, 14–19 January 1944

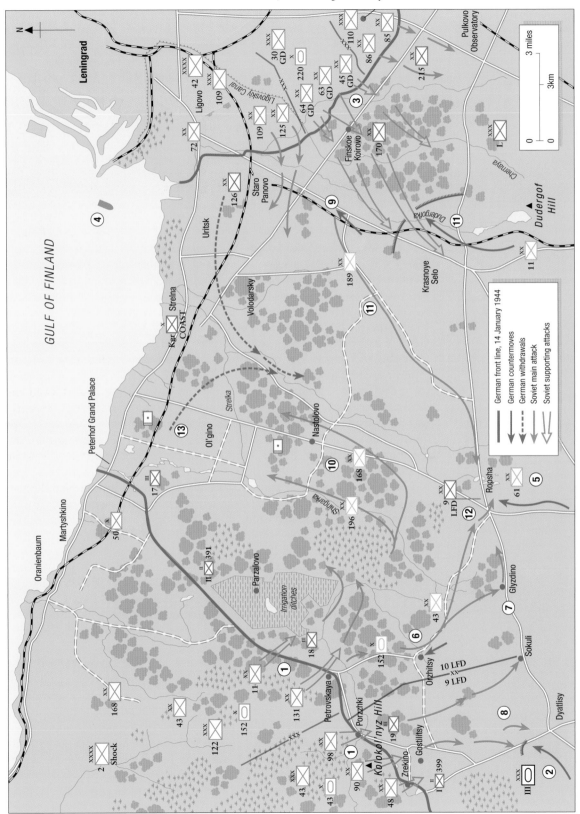

If that succeeded, the plan envisioned cutting off the Pogost'e salient and a direct assault on Leningrad. However, *Parkplatz* required at least one Panzer and seven infantry divisions to execute and these forces were already committed to Operation *Zitadelle* against the Kursk salient. Hitler was lukewarm about *Parkplatz*, but said that forces could be transferred to Küchler from Heeresgruppe Mitte after *Zitadelle* was completed.

However, *Zitadelle* was a failure, which ended any possibility of another German offensive near Leningrad. After Kursk, the Stavka authorized Govorov and Meretskov to initiate limited offensives to reduce German artillery interdiction of the one railway line into Leningrad and to set the stage for a decisive end to the siege. Govorov and Meretskov planned another simultaneous pincer attack on the Siniavino Heights, with the 67th Army attacking from the west and the 8th Army attacking from the east. The attack began at 0430hrs on 22 July with a two-hour artillery preparation. On the west side, General-Major Nikolai Simoniak, now in command of the reinforced 30th Guards Rifle Corps, attempted to penetrate XXVI AK's front line but failed to make any significant advance. On the east side, the 8th Army attacked with eight rifle divisions – enjoying a five: one combat superiority – against 5. Gebirgsjäger-Division, which put up a magnificent but costly defence. Once again, the Soviets committed large numbers of tanks into swampy terrain, where they became easy targets for German anti-tank gunners and the Tigers of s.Pz.Abt. 502. Lindemann reinforced the *Gebirgsjäger* with the 132. Infanterie-Division and Sturmgeschütz-Abteilung 912, bringing the Soviet attack to an abrupt halt. Nevertheless, the Stavka ordered the offensive to continue at a reduced level until 22 August, when it finally authorized a halt. For negligible gains, the Soviets had suffered another 79,937 casualties, including 20,890 dead or missing.

Perplexed by their lack of success, Govorov and Meretskov planned for a renewed effort in September, but decided upon narrower objectives and more precise use of forces. Simoniak's 30th Guard Rifle Corps would make a direct attack on the Siniavino Heights from the north, supported by much of the Front's aviation and artillery, while 8th Army made a supporting attack from the east. The German XXVI AK held the Siniavino Heights with the 11. and 290. Infanterie-Divisionen, while Lindemann had the bulk of the 28. Jäger-Division in reserve to support this sector. However, when Simoniak's rifle corps attacked on the morning of 15 September, advancing behind a creeping barrage instead of the usual two-hour artillery preparation, the Germans were caught by surprise and the guardsmen were soon atop the Siniavino Heights. Because of the speed of the Soviet victory, Lindemann was unable to reinforce this sector in time and resigned himself to the loss of the heights, but created a new defensive line just south of them. Meanwhile, the 8th Army's supporting attack on the east side of the salient was repulsed and unable to advance any further. After four days of fighting that cost another 70,000 casualties, the Stavka ended the offensive.

Simoniak's capture of the Siniavino Heights was one of the few bright spots in Soviet tactical performance on this front and greatly reduced the German artillery threat to the railway line running into Leningrad. It was now clear that the German blockade of Leningrad was reduced to a nominal level and Heeresgruppe Nord no longer had the ability to mount major offensives. Furthermore, the balance of forces on the northern front – as everywhere else – was quickly shifting against the Germans and Küchler began focusing more on improving his defensive options rather than restoring the siege. In order to shorten his lines and gain some reserves, Küchler received permission from Hitler to abandon the Kirishi salient on 1 October, which released the four divisions of XXVIII AK. He also gained permission to begin constructing the Panther Line, a new series of fortified positions running Narva–Pskov–Ostrov. Once completed, the Panther Line would provide Heeresgruppe Nord a refuge to retreat towards in the event of the Soviets succeeded in achieving a breakthrough around Leningrad.

The remainder of 1943 was relatively quiet around Leningrad, with the Soviets preparing to end the German siege once and for all, while the Germans steeled themselves for more Soviet offensives. After Italy's surrender, the Spanish withdrew their 250. Infanterie-Division from AOK 18 on 8 October, further weakening the German defences around Leningrad. In its place, a two-battalion Spanische Legion was formed and assigned to XXVIII AK.

THE SIEGE ENDS, 1944

Last winter of the siege

Despite the loss of the Siniavino Heights, the front lines had changed little in the past two years. Even in late 1943, German artillery still shelled Leningrad periodically and, unlike the rest of the Wehrmacht fighting on the Eastern Front, Heeresgruppe Nord had succeeding in fighting previous Soviet offensives to a standstill. However, Heeresgruppe Nord's defensive prowess led to the OKH transferring several of its veteran infantry divisions to other more threatened sectors and replacing them with low-quality Luftwaffe field divisions. Even the veteran s.Pz.Abt. 502 and its invaluable Tigers was sent to support AOK 16. With most of its armour, air support and veteran infantry gone, Heeresgruppe Nord was gradually transformed into a static defence formation, just as Soviet capabilities in the region were expanding with a new infusion of reinforcements.

At the start of January 1944, Lindemann's AOK 18 had 20 divisions in six corps, defended a front stretching from the Oranienbaum bridgehead, to the south side of Leningrad to Mga and then southwards to Novgorod on Lake Il'men. Although Lindemann had developed defences in depth, it was a very wide front for his troops to hold. On 13 December 1943, SS-Obergruppenführer Felix Steiner's III SS-Panzerkorps, consisting of the 9. and 10. Luftwaffe-Feld-Divisionen on the right and the 11. SS-Panzergrenadier-Division 'Nordland'

TOP

A German anti-tank team waits in ambush near Leningrad, armed with an early model RPzB-43 Panzerschreck rocket launcher. Introduced in 1943, the 88mm Panzerschreck was a reusable weapon that could knock out any Soviet tank up to 150–200m distant. Armeeoberkommando 18 formed Panzer-Zerstörer-Bataillone 477 and 478 in September 1943, each equipped with about 20 Panzerschrecke, to bolster its anti-tank defences. (HITM Archives)

BOTTOM

Two Soviet Maxim machine-gun teams from the 42nd Army's 110th Rifle Corps support the Soviet advance near Pushkin on 21 January 1944. The German 215. Infanterie-Division defending Pushkin soon found itself enveloped on three sides. (RIA Novosti)

and the 4. SS-Panzergrenadier-Brigade 'Nederland' on the left took over the Oranienbaum sector. The 'Nordland' was a relatively strong formation, but its Panzer battalion was not yet operational since the Panther tanks it had been issued were defective. Instead, the division had a battalion with 25 StuG III assault guns while the 'Nederland' had seven more. In the centre, L and LIV AK held the sector between Uritsk and Tosno with six divisions, XXVI AK held Mga with six divisions and XXVIII and XXXVIII AK held the Volkhov with five divisions. Armeeoberkommando 18 had only a single unit in reserve – the 61. Infanterie-Division, deployed near Krasnogvardeisk.

Meanwhile, Govorov was planning a new offensive to end the siege once and for all. For the first time, the Soviets sought operational surprise; instead of just launching another offensive against Mga, Govorov intended to launch his main effort from Oranienbaum, which had been a quiet sector for over two years. Beginning in November 1943, the KBF started transferring the rebuilt 2nd Shock Army (now under Fediuninskiy) from Leningrad to

Oranienbaum. By early January 1944, Fediuninskiy had five rifle divisions, 13 artillery regiments and three tank units massed in the Oranienbaum bridgehead. German intelligence detected this transfer and Lindemann did what he could to strengthen this sector. The two weak Luftwaffe field divisions were reinforced with two infantry battalions from the reliable 170. Infanterie-Division, two assault gun batteries, two *Panzerjäger* batteries and plenty of flak guns. The OKH also sent Panther Detachment 'Maeckert', formed from I/Panzer-Regiment 29, to provide additional anti-tank defences around Oranienbaum. (These Panthers had defective engines and were only semi-mobile.) Steiner used these additional forces to conduct several spoiling attacks in late December, but they were too weak to disrupt the upcoming Soviet offensive.

Govorov's plan directed the 2nd Shock Army to attack out of the Oranienbaum bridgehead and link up with General-Colonel Ivan Maslennikov's 42nd Army, which would attack westwards out of Leningrad towards Krasnoye Selo. He hoped that this surprise attack would cause Küchler to shift his scant reserves to that sector, thereby weakening his forces on the Volkhov. Meretskov would then attack with the 8th, 54th and 59th armies, to smash in the weakened right flank of AOK 18. Given a substantial edge in artillery, tanks and air support, Govorov and Meretskov expected a fairly quick German collapse followed by a full-bore pursuit to the Panther Line. For the first time, Govorov also coordinated with the increasingly effective partisan units operating in the German rear areas, hoping to disrupt German supply lines at the critical moment.

Soviet troops from the 110th Rifle Corps rush into the Catherine Palace in Pushkin on 24 January 1944. The liberation of Pushkin, Krasnoye Selo and the Peterhof effectively marked the end of the siege of Leningrad. (Author's collection)

Breakout from Oranienbaum, January

At 0935hrs on 14 January 1944, the 2nd Shock Army began a 65-minute artillery preparation against the 9. and 10. Luftwaffe-Feld-Divisionen on the eastern side of the Oranienbaum bridgehead. Thirteen army artillery regiments were joined by the battleships *October Revolution* and *Marat* and heavy railway guns and together they fired an incredible 104,000 rounds at the hapless Luftwaffe troops. Then, the 43rd and 122nd rifle corps attacked the boundary between the two Luftwaffe divisions with five rifle divisions and two tank brigades. Three more rifle divisions and another tank brigade stood behind them, poised to exploit the breakthrough. This was one of the best set-piece Soviet operations of the entire siege and yet, the assault troops succeeded in advancing only three to four kilometres by nightfall. Just before the attack, Steiner sent part of Nordland's pioneer battalion to strengthen the Luftwaffe-held sector and these stalwart troops fought a desperate delaying action that slowed down the Soviet steamroller. Nevertheless, both Luftwaffe divisions were badly hurt and as darkness fell, Fediuninskiy committed the 152nd Tank Brigade and two tank regiments, which advanced four more kilometres during the night. Steiner sent Nordland's reconnaissance battalion and one Panzergrenadier battalion to establish blocking positions on the west side of the Soviet penetration but they failed to deflect Fediuninskiy from his real objective: Ropsha. On the second day of the offensive, Fediuninskiy widened his penetration by crushing the remnants of the 10. Luftwaffe-Feld-Division, although German artillery fire inflicted heavy losses on the Soviet infantry.

While Fediuninskiy was clawing his way through III SS-Panzerkorps' lines, the 42nd Army used its 18th and 23rd breakthrough artillery divisions to reduce the defences of L AK's three divisions with a fierce artillery bombardment on 14 January, which increased to 220,000 shells fired in a

90-minute period on the morning of 15 January. These two formations fired a concentrated barrage from over 900 guns and mortars, including 48 203mm, 120 152mm howitzers and 88 multiple rocket launchers against a 15km-wide sector. Even the single 406mm gun at the Toksovo test range joined the barrage, firing several rounds at the Pulkovo Heights. After the German front-line positions were thoroughly pulverized, the 42nd Army attacked at 1100hrs with nine rifle divisions from the 30th Guard, 109th and 110th rifle corps. Once again Simoniak's 30th Guards Rifle Corps, transferred from the Siniavino sector, made the main effort. Simoniak's three guards rifle divisions attacked the 170. Infanterie-Division on the Pulkovo Heights and succeeded in advancing three to four kilometres on the first day, but German counterfire soon reduced the Soviet advance to the usual crawl. Maslennikov's objective was to capture Krasnoye Selo, then Ropsha.

Lindemann committed his only reserve, the 61. Infanterie-Division, to plug the gap caused by the disintegration of the 10. Luftwaffe-Feld-Division and to hold Ropsha. He also ordered Steiner to counterattack into the flank of the Soviet penetration with Nordland. These German efforts briefly slowed 2nd Shock Army but on 17 January, Fediuninskiy committed a mobile group of tanks, motorized infantry and self-propelled artillery under Colonel Andrei Oskotsky, which pushed through the flimsy German line. Maslennikov also committed his armour and the two Soviet pincers began to close inexorably on the German troops holding the area around the Peterhof and Uritsk. On 18 January, the 42nd Army captured the Dudergof Heights, just outside Krasnoye Selo. Küchler wanted to gain additional reserves by withdrawing from Mga, but Hitler refused because he feared it would precipitate a general withdrawal to the Panther Line.

Instead, the OKH belatedly sent reinforcements to buttress Heeresgruppe Nord but Soviet partisans succeeded in disrupting railway lines north of Pskov at the critical moment, impeding the German response. Oskotsky's tanks scored a clean breakthrough on 19 January and at 2100hrs, troops from the 2nd Shock Army and the 42nd Army linked up near Ropsha. Both the 126. Infanterie-Division and part of the L AK's artillery were now isolated, but many German troops were able to escape southwards through the thin Soviet lines during the night of 19/20 January, though without their heavy equipment. Much of the German artillery that had been shelling Leningrad for over two years was abandoned in the woods near the Peterhof. After six days of fighting, the Leningrad Front had restored ground communications with the Oranienbaum bridgehead and had unhinged the left wing of AOK 18's main defence line.

While Govorov was tearing open the German left, Meretskov went to work on the German right. General-Lieutenant Ivan Korovnikov's 59th Army was assigned to attack General Kurt Herzog's XXXVIII AK on the same sector of the Volkhov south of Chudovo where the 2nd Shock Army had failed in January 1942. However, the situation was far different two years later, since the Germans were much weaker and the Soviets more experienced. After another massive artillery bombardment, Korovnikov attacked with six rifle divisions in his first echelon. Further south, a Soviet mobile group daringly crossed the ice of Lake Il'men and established a bridgehead south of Novgorod, which greatly unnerved Herzog. By January 1944, XXXVIII AK was the weakest formation in AOK 18, consisting of only the depleted 28. Jäger-Division, the inexperienced 1. Luftwaffe-Feld-Division and the 2. Lettische SS-Freiwilligen-Brigade.

Forced to divert forces to deal with the incursion across Lake Il'men and with its thinly manned front pounded by massed artillery, XXXVIII AK began to fall apart on 15 January. Part of the stalwart 28. Jäger-Division was overwhelmed, with the remainder retreating into Novgorod. Confronted with a 20km-wide gap in his front between the remnants of XXXVIII and XXVIII AK around Lyuban, Lindemann began shifting further units south from the Mga sector. Meretskov ordered the 54th Army to conduct fixing attacks on the XXVIII AK that succeeded in preventing any further reinforcements being sent to restore the German line near Novgorod.

The remnants of the 28. Jäger-Division and the 1. Luftwaffe-Feld-Division were far too weak to hold the city. Once Soviet pincers were about to envelop Novgorod from both sides, Lindemann promptly asked the OKH for permission to abandon the city and Hitler reluctantly agreed. Although XXXVIII AK troops temporarily escaped, many were lost in the Soviet pursuit over the next few days. On the morning of 20 January, the Soviet 59th Army entered the deserted city of Novgorod. With his left and right flanks in tatters and the Soviet advance gathering steam, it was clear to Lindemann that not only was the siege of Leningrad over, but that AOK 18 was no longer capable of holding its remaining positions near Leningrad and that retreat was now inevitable.

AFTERMATH

WITHDRAWAL TO THE PANTHER LINE

After the success of the initial breakthrough attacks, Govorov and Meretskov turned to the task of defeating AOK 18 by means of envelopment. Maslennikov's 42nd Army was ordered to push south towards Krasnogvardeisk and Pushkin, while Fediuninskiy's 2nd Shock Army advanced south-west towards Kingisep. Korovnikov's 59th Army continued to advance westwards towards Luga, but was slowed more by the swampy terrain than the Germans. The Soviet 67th and 54th armies also joined in the general offensive, trying to pin the German forces around Mga and Lyuban. By 21 January, Küchler realized that AOK 18 could no longer hold a continuous front. He asked Hitler for permission to begin tactical withdrawals to shorten his line and gain reserves, but was refused. Without permission, Lindemann abandoned Mga and the positions near Siniavino, freeing up one division that was sent to block the 42nd Army advance, but it was too late.

The Soviet offensive gathered speed as the 42nd Army enveloped German forces in Pushkin and reached the outskirts of Krasnogvardeisk. Both s.Pz.Abt. 502 and the 12. Panzer-Division had been sent to stiffen AOK 18, but had been delayed by partisan attacks on the railway line. Yet if Lindemann's forces could hold out for a few more days, enough armour might be available to counterattack and restore the situation. The remnants of L AK made a stand at Krasnogvardeisk, with the help of four Tiger tanks and succeeded in repulsing the first attacks by 42nd Army. However, the Soviet steamroller was in full stride and Kampfgruppe Meyer quickly found itself encircled and lost 11 Tiger tanks on 21 January. Maslennikov's 42nd Army suffered heavy losses but finally fought its way into Krasnogvardeisk on 26 January. Despite Hitler's refusal to authorize a withdrawal to the Panther Line, Lindemann continued withdrawing without orders. Four days later, the spearheads of 2nd Shock Army and 42nd Army reached the Luga River.

Although AOK 18 was in a wretched state by late January, the Soviet pursuit after their great victory near Leningrad failed to destroy any major German units or capture large numbers of prisoners. When it became clear that Küchler would withdraw all the way to the Panther Line, Hitler relieved him of command on 29 January and replaced him with Generaloberst Walter Model. Model attempted to form hedgehogs around Narva and Luga and to launch small counterattacks to stem the Soviet tide, but he succeeded only in delaying the inevitable. Oberst Wengler's regiment succeeded in stopping the

Soviet spearheads outside Narva, but Luga fell on 12 February. Unable to maintain positions on the Luga River, Model finally began a general withdrawal to the Panther Line on 17 February. Yet by the time that Soviet forces reached the Panther Line, they were too depleted from weeks of fighting and were unable to penetrate the German defences. Once again, Meretskov began the laborious process of bringing up his artillery and rebuilding depleted rifle units. During January–February 1944, AOK 18 suffered 36,677 casualties, while the Soviet forces involved in the offensive had suffered 277,744 casualties. Heeresgruppe Nord had gained a respite, but not a reprieve.

In 47 days of fighting, the Leningrad and Volkhov fronts advanced 300km and shattered the previously impregnable defences of Heeresgruppe Nord. The siege of Leningrad, having lasted 880 days, was over. However, the agony of Leningrad's defenders was not. In May 1945, Stalin proclaimed Leningrad as one of five 'Hero Cities' and promised to rebuild the city promptly, but in fact, reconstruction efforts lagged for years. Stalin was embarrassed by the true scale of Soviet casualties at Leningrad and ordered a crackdown on details about the siege. Rather than honouring Soviet suffering and heroism on the Leningrad front, Stalin sought to conceal it. Furthermore, Stalin was suspicious of Zhdanov and his Leningrad clique and conducted his final purge in 1950, resulting in the arrest and execution of many of those who had organized the defence in 1941.

ANALYSIS OF THE SIEGE

Hitler had intended to demolish Leningrad as both a symbol and a centre of Soviet power, but he accomplished neither. Thus in strategic terms, the German effort against Leningrad was a failure. Yet in operational terms, the German siege of Leningrad effectively isolated three Soviet armies for over two years and forced six other armies to conduct repeated costly frontal assaults to try and end the siege. In January 1944, the Red Army had to mass the equivalent of over 60 divisions in the Leningrad–Volkhov area to dislodge 20 German divisions and still failed to encircle and destroy a single one of them. Total Soviet military casualties on the Leningrad and Volkhov fronts during the siege were at least 1.5 million, including 620,000 dead or captured. Furthermore, the siege cost the lives of about one million Soviet civilians in Leningrad and prevented the city's industries from participating fully in the Soviet war effort until mid-1944.

Yet despite causing massive death and suffering, the Germans failed in their efforts to push Leningrad's defenders to the breaking point. Indeed, it does not seem that AOK 18 and Luftflotte I made a serious effort to crush Leningrad when it had the opportunity. Except for brief surge periods, the air and artillery bombardments were more of a harassing nature than a serious effort to 'level' the city – in fact, not a single major target in the city was destroyed. Compared with the attacks on Stalingrad in August 1942, where the Luftwaffe put up to 600 bomber sorties per day over a city, Luftflotte I rarely attacked Leningrad with more than a couple of dozen bombers. Similarly, too much of the artillery bombardment was conducted with obsolete French weapons firing shells that were too small to smash down large buildings. Both the OKH and Küchler demonstrated a serious lack of imagination in failing to implement any measures either to speed up the siege or eliminate critical targets in the

Leningrad area. Given the natural outbreak of typhus and cholera inside Leningrad in 1942, the Germans might have considered contaminating the Neva River – the only source of fresh water for the trapped population – which could have resulted in catastrophic collapse within a few weeks.

Heeresgruppe Nord also failed utterly in efforts to isolate Leningrad by severing the Soviet logistic links across Lake Ladoga. Luftwaffe and artillery attacks harassed Soviet supply operations, but never came close to shutting them down. During winter, AOK 18 was unwilling to send its single ski battalion onto the ice of Lake Ladoga to harass the ice road, even though many convoys were poorly guarded at first. Finally, the German failure to crush the weakly held Oranienbaum bridgehead tied down a complete corps for two years of pointless static warfare and then left the Soviets a valuable springboard for future offensive operations. In spite of shortages of troops, Küchler had the forces on hand in July 1942 to mount a quick three-division attack on Oranienbaum that could have overwhelmed the bridgehead.

In spite of their operational mistakes which cost them victory at Leningrad, the German tactical performance on the defence was impressive – perhaps one of the best of the war by any army. On the 50m-high Siniavino Heights, German troops held off about 250,000 Soviet troops for 384 days and inflicted over 400,000 casualties. In comparison, German forces defending atop the 516m-high Monte Cassino massif held off 100,000 Allied troops for 123 days and inflicted about 20,000 casualties.

Soviet operational performance at Leningrad was badly hindered in 1941/42 by constant political interference from Stalin and his Kremlin cronies. Stalin wanted this symbolic city relieved as quickly as possible and paid little heed to Meretskov's professional arguments that proper logistic preparations were essential to success. Once offensives began, Meretskov was often forced to commit his reserves too early and to push for territorial objectives, rather than methodically enlarge the breach by eliminating German strongpoints. Tactically, Soviet forces suffered badly in 1942 from lack of combined arms operations, particularly in failure to use engineers and artillery properly to overcome German strongpoints.

However, Soviet leaders learned quickly at Leningrad and their effectiveness increased over the course of the siege. Yet even during the successful offensive in January 1944, the Soviets still suffered a 40 per cent casualty rate and lost 7.5 men for every German killed or captured. Indeed, the Soviet ability to regenerate combat power quickly was critical to their eventual success, particularly in the rapid rebuilding of the 2nd Shock Army (twice). Once Meretskov and Govorov learned from their earlier failures and were given the time and resources to prepare powerful set-piece offensives, the days of the siege were numbered.

THE BATTLEFIELD TODAY

A KV-1 tank monument at Ropsha marks the point where Soviet troops from Oranienbaum and Leningrad met on 19 January 1944. (Phil Curme Collection)

Modern St Petersburg has a large number of historical sites that reflect the 1941–44 siege of Leningrad. Starting inside the city, the Memorial Museum of Leningrad Defence and the Siege has a number of interesting displays and artefacts from the siege, including a German Pak 36 37mm anti-tank gun, German uniforms and period propaganda posters. Two other museums of interest are also the Military-Historical Museum of Artillery, Engineers and Signal Corps and the Central Naval Museum. Anchored next to the St Peter and Paul Fortress, the restored cruiser *Aurora* is open to visitors and has displays on her service in World War II. There is also a museum in the still-extant Smolny Institute, which was Zhdanov's headquarters throughout the siege. Anyone interested in getting a sense of the enormity of the loss of life suffered during the siege should visit the Piskaryovskoye Memorial Cemetery on the north-east side of the city, where some 420,000 civilians and 50,000 soldiers from the Leningrad Front are buried in mass graves. On the south side of the city, the Monument to the Heroic Defenders of Leningrad also has memorial displays.

On the north side of St Petersburg, there are a number of bunkers and trenches preserved near Agalatovo. The town of Novaya Ladoga, 50km north-east of St Petersburg, has a small museum with exhibits concerning the 'Road of Life' over Lake Ladoga as well as the operations of the Ladoga Flotilla. A small minesweeper from the flotilla is still preserved on display in the harbour. To the west of St Petersburg, there are monuments in Ropsha celebrating the link-up in January 1944 and the area around the Oranienbaum bridgehead still has some trenches and bunkers in existence. The Fort at Krasnaya Gorka remains military property but an effort is under way to create a museum and the TM-3-12 and TM-1-180 railway guns were still there in 2008.

There are a large number of historical sights east of the city, where most of the fighting occurred in 1942/43. In particular, the Breakthrough of the Siege of Leningrad museum at Marino on the Neva River has a large diorama depicting the Soviet breaking of the blockade in January 1943. Also nearby is the Neva River bridgehead (Nevsky Pyatachok) near Dubrovka, which has a memorial to the troops lost in this tiny foothold in 1942/43. Further up the Neva is the town of Shlissel'burg and the Oreshek fortress, still in existence but difficult to reach. Atop the Siniavino Heights there are a number of memorials and displays.

BIBLIOGRAPHY

Primary sources
Captured German Records held at NARA:
T-311: Heeresgruppe Nord
T-312: AOK 11, 16 and 18
T-314: XXVI, XXXVIII, XXXIX, XLI and L AK
T-354: SS-Polizei-Division, III SS-Panzer-Korps

Other sources
Achkasov, V. I., and N. B. Pavlovich, *Soviet Naval Operations in the Great Patriotic War 1941–45* (Naval Institute Press: Annapolis, MD, 1981)

Bergström, Christer, and Andrey Mikhailov, *Black Cross/Red Star*, Volumes 1, 2 and 3 (Pacifica Military History: Pacifica, California, 2001/2006)

Glantz, David M., *The Battle for Leningrad, 1941–1944* (University Press of Kansas: Lawrence, KS, 2002)

——, *Atlas of the Battle of Leningrad: Soviet Defense and the Blockade, July 1941 – December 1942* (Carlisle, PA, 2001)

——, *Atlas of the Battle of Leningrad: Breaking the Blockade and Liberation, 1 January 1943–15 July 1944* (Carlisle, PA, 2001)

Haupt, Werner, *Heeresgruppe Nord* (Schiffer Military History: Atglen, PA, 1997)

Jones, Michael, *Leningrad: State of Siege* (Basic Books: New York, 2008)

Kleinfeld, Gerald R., and Lewis A. Tambs, *Hitler's Spanish Legion* (Hailer Publishing: St Petersburg, FL, 2005)

Lubbeck, William, *At Leningrad's Gates: The Combat Memoirs of a Soldier with Heeresgruppe Nord* (Casemate: Philadelphia, 2006)

Margry, Karel and Ron Hogg, *The Siege of Leningrad*, After the Battle, No. 123, 2004

Manstein, Erich von, *Lost Victories* (Presidio Press: Novato, CA, 1986)

Meretskov, Kirill A., *On the service of the nation* (Politizdat: Moscow, 1968)

Mueller-Hillebrand, Burkhardt, et al. *The Retrograde Defense of Heeresgruppe Nord During 1944*, two volumes (Foreign Military Studies series, P-035, 1950)

Newton, Steven H., *Retreat from Leningrad: Heeresgruppe Nord 1944–1945* (Schiffer Military History: Atglen, PA, 1995)

Raus, Erhard, *Panzer Operations* (Da Capo Press: Cambridge, MA, 2003)

Salisbury, Harrison E., *The 900 Days: The Siege of Leningrad* (Da Capo Press: Cambridge, MA, 2)

Tieke, Wilhelm, Tragedy of the Faithful (J. J. Fedorowicz Publishing, Inc.: Winnipeg, 2001)

Wray, Timothy A., *Standing Fast: German Defensive Doctrine on the Russian Front During World War II, Prewar to March 1943*, Combat Studies Institute, Research Survey No. 5 (US Army Command and General Staff College: Ft Leavenworth, KS, 1986)

Websites
http://www.nortfort.ru/kgorka/index_e.html
An excellent website in English on the Krasnaya Gorka Fort.

INDEX